India

An Ancient Land, A New Nation

by Amita Vohra Sarin

सत्यमेव जयते

Dillon Press, Inc.   Minneapolis, Minnesota 55415

The official seal of India is pictured on the preceding page. The lions stand for power, courage, and confidence; The Wheel of Asoka is in the center; and underneath is written, "Truth alone triumphs."

Acknowledgments

The author wishes to thank the following people: Dr. Raj Sarin, Kiran Chandra, Sarla Prakash, Marilyn Mansfield, Sarla Vohra, Arun Vohra, Dr. K. Robbins, Dr. V.P. Singh, Malini Joglekar, Nirmala Rao, Gul Joshi, Dr. C. Singh, Suman Aggarwal, and Hameeda Siddiqui. She would also like to thank the staff of the Embassy of India, Washington, D.C., The Bureau of the Census, and *India West*, California, for their help and cooperation.

Special thanks are due to those who have graciously supplied photographs: Dr. D.K. Anand; Mr. Pradeet Wahi; the New York Philharmonic; and the India School, Maryland.

Cover photograph © Stella Snead

Library of Congress Cataloging in Publication Data

Sarin, Amita V..
   India: an ancient land, a new nation.

   (Discovering our heritage)
   Bibliography: p. 170.
   Includes index.
   Summary: Discusses the people, history, myths and legends, worship and celebrations, family life and food, school life, and sports of one of the world's most populous and diverse countries.
   1. India—Juvenile literature.   [1. India]
I. Title. II. Series.
DS407.S257   1985   954   84-10283
ISBN 0-87518-273-9

© 1985 by Dillon Press, Inc. All rights reserved

Dillon Press, Inc., 242 Portland Avenue South
Minneapolis, Minnesota 55415

Printed in the United States of America
1 2 3 4 5 6 7 8 9 10 92 91 90 89 88 87 86 85

Contents

	Fast Facts About India	4
	Map of India	6
1	Scientists and Snake Charmers	7
2	From Many Into One	25
3	A Peaceful, Tolerant People	51
4	Holy Books and Witty Fables	71
5	Sweets, Ceremonies, and Celebrations ...	85
6	Families, Homes, and Foods	99
7	A Respect for Learning	116
8	"Kabbaddi, Kabbaddi, Kabbaddi. . . ." ...	130
9	The Jet Generation	143
	Appendix A: Indian Embassies and Consulates in the United States and Canada	158
	Appendix B: The Languages of India	160
	Glossary	163
	Selected Bibliography	170
	Index	172

Fast Facts About India

Official Name: *Bharat*
Capital: New Delhi
Location: South central Asia. India extends southward into the Indian Ocean; it includes the Lakshadweep, Andaman, and Nicobar islands.
Area: 1,269,219 square miles (3,287,263 square kilometers); it stretches about 2,000 miles (3,200 kilometers) from north to south and about 1,700 miles (2,740 kilometers) from east to west; India has 4,252 miles (6,843 kilometers) of coastline, including the coasts of the island territories.
Elevation: *Highest*—Nanda Devi in the Himalayas, 25,645 feet (7,817 meters) above sea level. *Lowest*—sea level along the coasts.
Population: 723,533,000 in 1984; second largest in population; 570 persons per square mile (220 per square kilometer); *Distribution*—75 percent live in rural areas, 25 percent in cities.
Form of Government: Federal republic. *Head of State*—president (elected by the states); *Head of the Central Government*—prime minister (appointed by the ruling or majority party).
Some Important Products: cotton, jute, sugar, rice, tea, peanuts, coal, iron ore, copper, zinc, cotton yarn and cloth, paper, cement, aircraft, motor

scooters, electricity, brass and silver handicrafts

Basic Unit of Money: Rupee.

Languages: Hindi, along with English, is the official language, but fifteen languages are recognized by the Indian constitution.

Religions: Hinduism, Christianity, Islam, Sikhism, Jainism, Zoroastrianism.

Flag: Three horizontal stripes, of yellow-orange, white, and green. The Wheel of Asoka is in dark blue in the center of the flag.

National Anthem: "Jana-gana-mana" ("Thou Art the Ruler of the Minds of All People)".

Some Major Holidays: Diwali (November); Holi (March); Janam Ashtami (Krishna's birthday, August); Republic Day (January 26); Independence Day (August 15); Dassera (late October).

Indian States: Andhra Pradesh, Assam, Bihar, Gujarat, Haryana, Himachal Pradesh, Jammu and Kashmir, Karnataka, Kerala, Madhya Pradesh, Maharashtra, Manipur, Meghalaya, Nagaland, Orissa, Punjab, Rajasthan, Sikkim, Tamil Nadu, Tripura, Uttar Pradesh, West Bengal; *Indian Territories:* Andaman and Nicobar Islands, Aruncahal Pradesh, Chandigarh, Dadra and Nagar Haveli, Delhi, Goa-Daman-Diu, Lakshadweep, Mizoram, Pondicherry.

1. Scientists and Snake Charmers

While most Americans prepare for bed, the sun is rising on the other side of the world. In India it is already tomorrow. Seven hundred million Indians are getting ready for the new day.

On the globe, India lies even with Mexico, about halfway around from the United States. Its southern half pokes down from Asia into the Indian Ocean like an upside-down triangle, with its tip a few hundred miles north of the equator. The Lakshadweep Islands off its western coast and the Andaman and Nicobar islands in its eastern waters also belong to India. The island nation of Sri Lanka lies off the southern tip of India. Pakistan, Tibet, Russia, Nepal, Bangla Desh, Burma, and China are all close neighbors.

Besides China, no nation has more people than India. Every seventh person in the world today lives in crowded India. It has three times as many people as the United States, yet it has less than half the space. Still, India is a large country—the seventh largest in the world.

Like the United States, India has mountains, plains, forests, beaches, deserts, and swamps. Most

Photo © Stella Snead

India has many different kinds of landscapes and climates. The region may be cool and dry, as in the Himalayan Mountains of Kashmir (opposite, above); *hot and dry, as in the deserts of Rajasthan* (opposite, below); *or even hot and wet, as in the southern state of Kerala* (above).

people are surprised to learn this because they think of India as a hot, flat land. In fact, India is many lands in one. It is a union of twenty-two states and nine territories, as different from each other in geography and climate as is Alaska from Arizona and New Mexico from New York.

An Indian state is called a *pradesh.** Uttar Pradesh, Madhya Pradesh, Andhra Pradesh, and Himachal Pradesh are all names of states. Bengal, Assam, Gujarat, and Tamil Nadu are also Indian states. The

**Unless the glossary says otherwise, all foreign words in the text are Hindu words. They are said exactly as they are written.*

states are organized according to the language spoken by the majority of their people.

Fifteen major Indian languages are spoken in India today, along with hundreds of dialects, or local ways of speaking. These languages are all so different that Bengalis cannot understand Tamil and Gujaratis cannot speak Kashmiri. But millions of educated Indians all over the nation speak English, because for 200 years India was ruled by the British. English was the official language of India until 1965. *Hindi*, spoken by one third of the population, is now the official language of India, along with English.

Hindi is a language, but a *Hindu* is a person who follows *Hinduism*, a religion. Eight out of ten Indians are Hindus. As a result, India is often called *Hindustan*, the land of the Hindus, even though its official name is *Bharat*. Some say the names *Hindu* and *India* came from the river Indus, which flows through Pakistan. (Pakistan was once a part of India.)

However, the people of India do not all follow the same faith. With eighty million Muslims, India has the second largest Muslim population in the world. Sixteen million Christians, 12.5 million Sikhs, over 100,000 Zoroastrians, as well as many Buddhists, Jains, and Jews also live here. Two of India's presidents, so far, have been Muslim; and the latest is a Sikh. Like the United States, India is a secular nation;

that is, there is no state religion. Everyone is to practice his or her own faith.

Like the United States, India is a democratic country—a democracy with more people than any other. The people elect its leaders; every Indian citizen over the age of twenty-one has the right to vote. India's government is like that of Great Britain. The Indian Parliament has two houses, rather like our Senate and House. These are the *Rajya Sabha* (Council of States) and the *Lok Sabha* (House of the People). Members of Parliament are called MPs. The

Fifteen languages are recognized by the Indian Constitution (in addition to English). This advertisement shows English, Hindi, and Urdu lettering.

Lok Sabha has over 500 MPs, who are elected by the people of the states they represent. A council of ministers, headed by the prime minister, is formed from among the MPs of the majority party.

The Indian president does not have the same duties and powers as the American president. The prime minister is the actual leader of the Indian government. Although the central government is responsible for defense, foreign affairs, transportation, money, radio, and television, the states make many of their own decisions and laws.

A Quick Tour of India

Kashmir, India's northernmost state, is the home of the Cashmere goat which produces the famous, fine, Cashmere wool. People call Kashmir a paradise on earth because it has great beauty, with flowering meadows, orchards, waterfalls, and mountains.

Kashmir lies in the Himalayan Mountains. The Himalayas and other mountain ranges spread across fifteen hundred miles of India's northern borders. They are the tallest mountains in the world. Nanda Devi, India's highest peak, is over four miles high.

Himalaya means "abode [home] of the snows." These snows melt and feed the great Ganges River, India's largest waterway. Fifteen hundred miles long, the Ganges flows through a flat, broad plain below

Scientists and Snake Charmers

the mountains. The system of rivers that flows into the Ganges and Indus in Pakistan make this Indo-Gangetic plain one of the most fertile in the world. It is the heartland of India. Many people live there, in the states of Punjab, Haryana, Uttar Pradesh, Bihar, and Bengal. Some people grow sugar cane, wheat, and rice. Others live in the many busy cities.

West of this vast plain is the desert state of Rajasthan. Rajasthanis still ride on camels, especially in the sandier areas. In Rajasthan water is scarce and wells are sacred. It rains so seldom that in some desert villages children are excited and astonished to see drops of water come out of the sky!

How different is Cherrapunji, a town in the northeastern corner of India, which has the record for the world's heaviest rainfall. Here the ground is so fertile, the saying goes, that if you plant your foot in it, even it will grow! Thick, green bamboo forests cover the hilly states in the northeast.

Also in the northeast is the state of Assam. Assam is famous for the tea plantations that cover its gently sloping hills. Women with baskets strapped on their backs still pick tea leaves the old way—by hand. Yet, Assam has new industry, too—it produces half the nation's petrol (gasoline) and natural gas.

The Deccan plateau, in triangle-shaped southern India, is much drier and not as fertile as Assam or the

Indo-Gangetic plain. The conditions here are perfect for growing cotton. Many textile mills can be found in this region, particularly in Maharashtra.

Southern India has long been famous for its fine silks. Different kinds of silk are named after the towns where they are produced. While Bangalore, the capital of Karnataka state, is still known for its silk, it now produces the nation's airplanes and is a center for scientific research.

Science has also brought new fame to Kerala. Space rockets are launched from this small state on the southwest coast of India. Kerala was known for years as the land of spices. Ships brought traders from many countries to exchange gold and silver for Kerala's pepper, cloves, and cinnamon. Ancient Roman coins have even been found buried in southern India.

Coconut palms line the beautiful beaches of the south. Tamil Nadu, India's southernmost state, is famous for its huge temples of carved stone. Many pilgrims (people who journey to holy places) pass through it to Cape Comorin, at the tip of India's triangle. They pray at a temple perched on the rocks of the cape and wash themselves in the Indian Ocean.

Indian Seasons

Moisture from the Indian Ocean is picked up by winds called the *monsoons* as they blow towards

Scientists and Snake Charmers

India. These winds strike against the mountains and empty their clouds over the plains in rainstorms. Because the rains come after a long, hot summer, Indians look forward to the rainy season just as we wait for spring. Even the peacock, the national bird of India, spreads its splendid tail and dances at the sight of rain clouds.

But farmers wait for the monsoons in mixed hope and fear. Too much rain results in flooding; delayed rains mean drought. Thousands can either lose their lives and homes in floods or go hungry because of failed crops. The government has done much to help by building dams and canals, providing a steadier supply of water for farming.

After the rains comes winter, which is dry and mild in most parts of India. However, mountain winters are quite severe. Hill-dwellers there carry little earthenware stoves inside their clothes to keep warm. Nights on the northern plain can also get uncomfortably cold, because Indian homes are not centrally heated. But during the day Indians like to sit outdoors in the sunshine wrapped in shawls and sweaters.

People hide from the sun in the fierce heat of summertime. With temperatures climbing as high as 120° F., it can get so hot that you can fry an egg on the sidewalk! Those who can, escape to cool hill resorts.

Others stay indoors or in the shade during the day and sleep outdoors at night.

Indian Castes

Indian craft workers have long been admired for their skills. In the past, invaders often carried them away to other lands. The skills and secrets of each trade were passed down from father to son for generations. One had to be born to a weaver to be a weaver, or be a potter's child to be a potter. All Hindus were, and still are, divided by occupation into groups called *castes*. Today, even though you can change your occupation, you may never change your caste. You are born into it.

There are several hundred sub-castes (small groups) which fit into the four major castes. The highest caste are the *Brahmins*, or priests and scholars. Next are the *Kshatriyas*, the warriors and rulers. Then come the *Vaishyas*, or traders. Farmers and laborers are *Shudras*, the lowest caste. At the very bottom are the outcastes, who clean the streets and pick up dead animals.

Each caste had many strict rules for its members. You could not marry someone from a different caste. You could not eat a meal with someone from a lower caste. Outcastes had the strictest rules of all. These

Even though India becomes more modern every year, some tasks, such as farming, are often done in the traditional way.

people were supposed to live outside the village and not mix with the other castes. They were called untouchable.

Mahatma Gandhi, one of India's great leaders, did much to improve the lot of untouchables. He renamed them *Harijans*, or "people of God." Today, untouchability is forbidden by law. Many Harijans are landowners, doctors, and politicians. Caste is no longer as important as it used to be, especially in Indian cities.

But eight out of ten Indians live in India's half-a-million villages. In many villages, life goes on much as it did hundreds of years ago. Farmers still use oxen to plow their fields. Villagers still draw water from wells. Cow dung is used as fuel and to plaster the walls of the simple huts.

The New India

India's villages are changing. Almost half of them have electricity, and in many, electric pumps bring water to the fields. Tractors are taking the place of oxen in richer parts of the nation. In some states, television is being used to teach farmers ways of growing bigger, better crops. After work, many farmers and their families squat around the only TV set in the village to watch a special program which teaches them new ways of farming.

When India became independent, it had to import food for its 350 million people. Today, India grows its own food. Though the population has doubled, food production has almost tripled. American experts, especially a man named Norman Bourlag, helped Indian farmers to achieve this "Green Revolution" in the 1960s. Today the state of Punjab grows more food per acre than do American farms.

Indian manufacturing includes production of airplanes, ships, motor scooters, railroad cars, and trucks.

Still, many villagers are poor. Some do not have any land to farm. More and more poor people are going to the cities to look for work. Overcrowding in towns has become so bad that many people live on the sidewalks. Others live in overcrowded rooms, in slums, or in mud huts.

Not everyone in India's cities is this poor, however. Many Indians live quite comfortably in large homes with yards. The children in these homes eat and dress well, go to school, play with toys, and ride in cars. Those who cannot afford large homes and cars live in smaller homes and ride on two-wheel scooters. These people belong to the middle class. India has always been known as a land of very rich or very poor people. But now it has a middle class of 70 to 100 million people.

But whether they come from rich, poor, or middle-class families, children often enjoy the same things. Together they stand around the monkey man when he comes to their neighborhood. His monkeys, dressed as humans, perform tricks while the children laugh and clap.

Even adults stop to watch the snake charmer when he starts his show. He makes his snakes sway to the shrill music of his pot-bellied flute. Although snake charming is an ancient art, it is still a common sight on the streets of modern India.

City streets are crowded and noisy. Along with cars, scooters, and overfilled buses, there are many cyclists and people on foot. Cows often wander through the traffic or sleep on the sidewalks. Since cows are holy to the Hindus, no one bothers them. In older sections of town you can still see horse-drawn carriages, called *tongas*, and *rickshaws*, which are two-seat carriages pulled by a person.

In busy shopping areas called *bazaars* vendors call out their wares. Boys sell buttons and hairpins to

Some traditional entertainments include snake charmers (left) *and dancing monkeys* (above).

passers-by. Other boys sit on the sidewalks shining shoes for a living. Shoeshine boys squat near the long lines that form outside movie theaters.

India produces the largest number of movies in the world. Because Indians love the movies, cinema halls are often huge, with seating for hundreds and extra wide screens. But these days, those who can, buy their own video recorders and watch movies at home. Video movie libraries have sprung up in many city bazaars.

Places to Visit in India

Bombay, a port on the west coast, is India's Hollywood. It is the largest of India's 2,700 cities and towns and has both skycrapers and slums. Perfumed women travel in buses next to fish vendors who balance smelly fish in baskets on their heads.

Calcutta and Madras on the east coast are also major Indian ports. Together with Bombay and New Delhi, they make up India's "Big Four" cities. New Delhi, the capital, is India's second largest city. Next to New Delhi is Old Delhi. In fact, Delhi was destroyed and rebuilt at least eight times in the last three to four thousand years! Families picnic and children play among ruins of forts and tombs left behind by rulers from centuries past.

Near New Delhi is Agra, the site of the Taj Mahal. This is a magnificent white marble monument built more than 300 years ago by an emperor in memory of his queen. It is said that over 20,000 workers worked twenty-one years to build the Taj Mahal.

There are many *mahals* (palaces) in Rajasthan, land of *rajas* (kings). Jaipur, with its many palaces of pink sandstone, is known as the "pink city." The Lake Palace of Udaipur, also in Rajasthan, is now a hotel very popular with tourists. Many scenes from the James Bond movie *Octopussy* were filmed here.

India, the land of contrasts, often shows the old and the new side by side. This is a scene in Bombay.

Another favorite tourist city is Srinagar, the capital of Kashmir. It lies on the banks of a large lake, and many live on houseboats lined up near the shores. Other, smaller boats move back and forth, selling fruits and flowers to people living on the houseboats.

Places that tourists come to and modern Indian factories sometimes are in the same place. For example, Varanasi, on the banks of the Ganges, has fifteen hundred temples. It is perhaps one of the oldest living cities in the world and is visited by a million Hindu pilgrims every year. Varanasi also has a diesel locomotive factory.

India's Future

Until just a few years ago, India had to import many things that it needed. Today it builds ships in Vishakapatnam, trucks in Jamshedpur, and airplanes in Bangalore. Although only a small portion of its people work in factories, it ranks twelfth among the industrialized nations of the world. It exports many things, including machinery, to other lands. Although more than half its people cannot read or write, India has the third largest number of skilled workers in the world. Indian scientists have put a satellite in orbit, sent a man into space, and built nuclear power plants.

Yes, India is a land of opposites: a mixture of scientists and snake charmers, old and new, rich and poor, technology and tradition. It is an amazing nation, using new technology to solve age-old problems. Because of improved communication and travel, Indians are getting to know each other and other parts of their country better. Since independence, India has become a more united nation, one land instead of many lands in one. Though it is an ancient land, it is also a new nation. It has come a long way in a short time.

2. From Many Into One

The long story that is India's history could almost be a fairy tale. It includes evil kings and holy leaders; fabulous palaces and mud huts; terrible invaders and civil wars; colorful gods and goddesses and beautiful temples. The country that India is today is a blend of each new culture that was brought to the land. New people brought with them new ways, religions, and languages. They changed India and Indians in some way, and always, India changed them.

The First Indians

The story begins with Indians who lived in the Indus Valley region five thousand years ago. They lived in cities with brick houses, wide streets, storehouses for grain, and large public baths. How do we know about these long-ago people? Scientists called archeologists discovered the ruins of two ancient cities—Mohenjo Daro and Harappa—buried under mounds of earth. There they found some copper and bronze weapons and seals with an unknown kind of writing on them.

Why this Indus Valley civilization died we do not

know. We do know that in 1500 B.C., *Aryan* tribes wandered into India through the Himalayan passes in search of better pastures for their cattle. For centuries these tall, fair-skinned people had lived on the shores of the Caspian Sea. Some went west to Europe. Others came to India, bringing customs like the caste system with them.

At first, the Aryans hated the dark-skinned *Dravidians* who already lived in India, and tried to stay away from them. But over the years, the cultures of the two mixed. Today, there are no pure Aryans or Dravidians left. The Aryans forgot their own gods and began to pray to the gods of the Dravidians. The Dravidians began to speak the Aryan language, Sanskrit, and adopted the caste system. Gradually, this mixed religion—Hinduism—spread from the north to the very tip of southern India. Today the cow, which was once very important to the Aryans, is sacred to Hindus all over India. The *Vedas*, which were the hymns of the Aryans, are still recited in Sanskrit by dark-skinned Brahmins (priests) of the south. (Appendix B tells more about the Aryans and Sanskrit.)

When they first came, the Aryans had to clear the thick forests that covered the Indo-Gangetic plain. In time, they learned to farm the land and live in villages. Gradually, the people of India built cities and began to trade with each other. Small kingdoms began to develop on the plains. At the same time there were little independent republics where tribes elected their own leaders.

New Religions, New Invasions

The ruler of the Shakya tribe had a son named Gautama. Gautama was handsome and wealthy with a beautiful wife and baby son. Though his father tried to surround him with wonderful things, Gautama was not happy. He was sensitive and thoughtful; the sight of old age, disease, and death made him very sad. He promised himself that he would find a way to end all suffering. One night he left his sleeping family and went to the forest to think. He spent many years there, fasting and praying for enlightenment (knowledge of what is right).

Finally, one day as he sat deep in thought under a big tree (later called the *bodhi* or enlightenment tree), he found the answers to his questions. From that day on, he was called the *Buddha* or "enlightened one." For the rest of his life he traveled about, preaching that the only way to be happy was to stop wanting things. Unlike Hindu priests, Buddha treated members of the lower castes with respect and kindness. Many Hindus became his followers. For centuries,

A statue of Buddha reminds people of his reaching wisdom under the bodhi *tree.*

Buddhism was thought of as a form of Hinduism. Today it is a separate religion. Millions of Buddhists can be found all over the world.

At the same time as Buddha lived another great man called Mahavira. He preached *ahimsa*, which means nonviolence and respect to all living things, even insects. Today his followers are called *Jains*.

From Many Into One

Some time after the deaths of Buddha and Mahavira, Alexander, the great Greek conqueror, crossed into northwestern India. In 326 B.C. he fought a battle with Porus, one of the local Indian kings. Porus had a huge army of elephants, while Alexander's army went on foot. Alexander told his soldiers to shoot down the men riding on top of the animals. The riderless elephants panicked and trampled on their own soldiers. Porus was defeated.

Alexander was eager to be master of India, but he had been fighting battles ever since he had left Greece. His tired, homesick men refused to go any further. Alexander was forced to turn back, leaving generals behind to govern his conquered territories. These generals ruled Persia and Afghanistan for many centuries. But they did not rule long over northern India.

The First Indian Empires

In Alexander's time, India was made up of several little states with independent rulers. The first man to unite many of these kingdoms into one large empire was Chandragupta Maurya. He even defeated Seleucus, one of Alexander's generals, and married his daughter. Chandragupta's descendants ruled this empire for many years. They were called the Mauryan kings.

The greatest Mauryan king—indeed, the greatest of all Indian emperors—was Chandragupta's grandson, Asoka, who ruled from 268 to 231 B.C. Asoka was a war-loving king who wanted to increase his empire. But after the terrible battle of Kalinga, where 100,000 people lost their lives, he was overcome with remorse and regret.

Asoka swore never to go to war again, and a few years later became a Buddhist. He had the sayings of Buddha and his own philosophy carved on pillars and placed all over India. He told his people to be tolerant of other religions (that is, to let them worship as they pleased). Asoka sent missionaries to other countries to preach Buddhism. His own sister sailed to Ceylon (Sri Lanka) with a branch of the bodhi tree, which still flourishes there.

Four huge stone lions sit back to back on top of one of the Asokan pillars. These lions are now the official seal of the Indian government and are stamped in gold on Indian passports. Asoka's wheel, the Wheel of Law, carved on many of his pillars, has a place of honor in the center of the Indian flag.

It is said that in A.D. 52, Saint Thomas, one of Jesus Christ's apostles, brought a new religion—Christianity—to India. He established several Christian churches on the Malabar coast (which is now Kerala). There, Christians lived alongside Jews; a group of Jewish immigrants had arrived in 586 B.C. and settled in the same area of southern India.

The Gupta Rulers

By this time, the ways of the north and the south had mixed quite a bit. Even Tamil kings of the far south performed ceremonies in Sanskrit, the language of the north. One such ceremony was a horse sacrifice. A white horse was blessed, and then allowed to roam for a year before it was killed to please the gods. A king's followers went after the horse. All the land that the horse wandered over belonged to the king who had sent it out, unless the owner of the land stopped the horse. Then the landowner and the king's soldiers fought until someone had won the right to the land.

This was how Samudragupta, a fourth-century king in northern India, expanded his kingdom. Soon he ruled over most of northern India. Samudragupta was not just a warrior; he loved music and poetry, too. One of the coins he had made shows him playing a musical instrument. His descendants also ruled for many years and loved learning. They were called the Gupta kings.

Samudragupta's son, Vikramaditya, became the greatest Gupta monarch. At his court were Sanskrit scholars, poets, philosophers, and mathematicians. Books on astronomy and mathematics were written. We know now that algebra really began in India. The decimal system and the numerals we use today also started there. All these were later taken west by Arabs. This became known as the golden age of the Guptas. But it did not last forever.

In A.D. 500, Central Asian tribes called the Huns broke into India. They were tough horsemen who could sleep in the saddle and eat raw meat. Cruel and fierce, they robbed, killed, or burned everything in their way. Indians trembled at their very name. The Huns ruled India for seventy years, after which they were defeated by an Indian king. In time, they too settled in the land and were absorbed among the people of India.

In A.D. 606 another emperor rose to power. His name was Harsha. Though Harsha was a brave soldier, he was also a talented writer who wrote three plays. Harsha was a kind man. Every five years or so, he gave away everything he had—clothes, money, and jewels—to the poor. Once he had to borrow an old garment from his sister because he had nothing left to wear!

During Harsha's reign, a new religion—*Islam*—was founded in the Arabian desert by a man named Muhammed. Followers of Islam are called Muslims

From Many Into One

or Muhammedans. Islam spread rapidly among the Arab and other countries of the Middle East, including Persia. The Muslims thought it was their duty to force the whole world to become Muslims. In A.D. 712, an Arab army occupied Sindh (now in Pakistan) bringing Islam to India. But they were stopped there by the Rajput kings, who united against them and prevented them from marching further into India.

The Rajputs were brave warriors who had ruled much of western and middle India for many years. They were descendants of tribes that came in with the Huns. When a Rajput went to battle he wanted to either win or die. Rajput women were equally fearless. If their men were defeated, they prepared a large fire and jumped into it so that they would not be captured by the enemy.

However, Rajput princes did not always get along with each other, and soon after their victory started fighting among themselves. Since the time of the Hun invasion, India had been left more or less alone for five hundred years. Hindus did not feel the need to be strong and united.

This is why, when an Afghan ruler, Mahmud of Ghazni, started raiding India, there was no one to stop him. He raided India seventeen times between 997 and 1030. He loved to destroy Hindu temples. Hindus have never forgiven him for ruining the magnificent temple of Somnath. Here, 50,000 people were killed, and masses of gold, silver, and jewels were carried away.

The raids of Mahmud were followed by those of the Prince of Ghor, also from Afghanistan. This time the Rajput princes decided to fight together under Prithviraj Chauhan, a hero of Indian history. They defeated the Afghan army in 1191, but unfortunately Prithviraj was killed in a battle with Ghori in 1192. The swift Asian horses won against the slow elephants of the Rajputs. The Muslims became the rulers of northern India.

Five Hundred Years of Islam

Muhammad of Ghori left behind a very clever slave, Qutab-ud-din Aibak, who became sultan of Delhi after Ghori's death. Qutab and his successors were known as the Slave Dynasty. They built a tall tower called the Qutab Minar in Delhi. Children still love to climb up the steep steps to the very top.

The Delhi sultans held power for three centuries. A series of kings did manage to conquer more land to the south. But in southern India there was a powerful empire called *Vijaynagar*. It was known for its well-planned cities, temples, and palaces. Krishna Deva Raya was a famous Vijaynagar king who encouraged

The Qutab Minar still stands in Delhi.

poets and writers at his court to write in both Telegu, the language of his kingdom, and Sanskrit. The Hindus of the south tried to protect their ways, since the north had been taken over by the Muslims.

Nevertheless, by now, Islam and Hinduism had mixed in many ways. Islam was no longer a "foreign" religion; many Indians had converted to it. Individuals such as Kabir and Nanak did much to bring the two religions together.

Kabir was a Muslim weaver born in 1440. He preached to the common folk in simple language. He wanted them to think more of spiritual things and less about the things on earth. His sayings are quoted even today.

Nanak was born in Punjab in 1469. At first he was considered a lazy dreamer, but soon he started preaching, to Hindus and Muslims alike. He said there was only one God and that all people were equal. His followers today are called Sikhs and he is revered as their first *guru* (teacher).

In 1498, during Nanak's lifetime, Vasco da Gama, a Portuguese sailor, reached India. For years Europeans had been looking for a sea route to India. Europeans loved Indian spices and silks, but had had no way to go to India to buy them themselves. They were forced to rely on Arab traders, who charged high prices for Indian goods. Vasco da Gama filled his ships with Indian spices and sold the spices at high profits in Europe. Later the Portuguese took over Goa, south of Bombay, and kept it until 1961.

The Mughal Rulers

Meanwhile, another invader from Afghanistan was looking greedily at the wealth of India. He was Babur, who was then the ruler of Kabul. With the

From Many Into One

help of Turkish guns and Mongolian horses, Babur defeated the sultan of Delhi at the battle of Panipat in 1526.

Babur settled at Agra, near Delhi. But soon he was homesick for Kabul. He built beautiful gardens with fruit trees and running water to remind him of his favorite garden in Kabul. Babur died after ruling only four years, but he started the Mughal empire in India, where his sons and grandsons would rule for 200 years.

Akbar means "great," and Akbar, Babur's grandson, was the greatest Mughal emperor. He became king at the age of thirteen. Because he preferred to hunt and play, Akbar never learned to read and write. But he surrounded himself with wise counselors, poets, and musicians. He had a library with 24,000 books. Though Akbar was a Muslim, he married Rajput princesses, who were Hindus. He also abolished the *jizya*, a tax that had to be paid by non-Muslims. It was his tolerance of other religions that helped knit most of India into one great empire.

For many years Akbar had no heir. Finally, he sought the blessing of a holy man who lived in a village near Agra. The man predicted correctly that Akbar would have three sons. In gratitude, Akbar built a new capital at the village, Sikri, that had magnificent red sandstone buildings.

Akbar's grandson, Shah Jahan, loved precious stones. He had a beautiful throne called the Peacock Throne built for himself. It was studded with rubies and emeralds and was topped by the Kohinoor, a world-famous diamond. But Shah Jahan is remembered most for building the Taj Mahal. This beautiful white marble monument was built in memory of his beloved wife, who died quite young. Later, Shah Jahan was put in prison by his own son, Aurangzeb, and died eight years later, still gazing at the Taj Mahal.

Aurangzeb was a hard, joyless man. He was a strict Muslim, and throughout his reign was very hard on those who were not. He started collecting the jizya tax again and fought many enemies, both Hindu and Sikh. One of them was a Hindu named Shiva ji.

Shiva ji was a brave Maratha chieftain who lived among the hills of the Western Ghats (mountains on the southwest coast of India). Though he had only a small band of horsemen, the large Mughal armies were unable to defeat him. He dodged in and out of the hills for twenty years. Finally Aurangzeb invited him to come to Agra and then imprisoned him. Shiva ji escaped hidden in a large basket of sweets. As you can imagine, Shiva ji is a great hero to the Hindus.

After the death of Aurangzeb in 1707, the Mughal empire fell apart, and soon the Marathas were

The Taj Mahal was built by Shah Jahan in memory of his favorite wife, who died at an early age.

controlling large parts of it. By this time, the British had come to India. A group of English traders had formed the East India Company in 1603 and had set up trading posts in little villages that later became the cities of Bombay, Calcutta, and Madras.

The European Influence

The British came as traders but stayed on as rulers, controlling India for two hundred years. They helped Indian kings fight one another, and, in time, took over their kingdoms. They taxed Indians heavily to get rich fast. This made the once-rich regions of Bengal and Bihar very poor. Finally, in 1857, there was a big revolution. It started with Indian soldiers in the British army, but many Indian leaders joined in. One of these was the queen of Jhansi, who put on men's clothes and led her people to battle against the British.

This revolt was sternly put down and India was made an official part of the British Empire. The result was a more just government for Indians. Roads, railways, and telegraph services soon linked various parts of India. By and by, many educated Indians had a common language—English. Without really meaning to, the British had knit the Indians into a unified people. Now the Indians—Hindu, Sikh, and Muslim alike—had a common enemy—the British.

Mohandas (Mahatma) Gandhi, whose leadership and nonviolent methods of protest helped India become an independent nation, was assassinated in 1948.

Indians wanted to govern themselves. They organized marches, meetings, and protests against the British. At one such meeting in 1919, in a garden in Amritsar, a British general had his troops fire on an unarmed crowd. A thousand people were killed. This shocked even the British and made Indians even more stubborn in their demand for self-government.

Mohandas Gandhi, a young Indian lawyer educated in England, was the leader of India's freedom struggle. Since he was against bloodshed and violence, he taught Indians an unusual way of fighting. It was called non-cooperation. He told his fellow citizens to quit British jobs and refuse to buy British goods. In those days, Indian cotton was taken to England and made into cloth to be resold in India at high prices. Gandhi stopped wearing Western clothes; instead, he wore clothes made from a simple cloth which he spun himself. He urged other Indians to burn British cloth and follow his example. To this day, members of the Indian Congress wear clothes made of this homemade cotton.

India's fight for freedom lasted almost thirty years. At first, Hindus and Muslims were united against the British. Then a group of Muslims began to demand a separate Muslim state called Pakistan. When India finally became free it was divided into two countries. During this partition, hundreds of thousands killed one another in angry fighting. Fifteen million became refugees. Many blamed Gandhi for agreeing to the division of India. Some felt he was favoring the Muslims. In 1948, an assassin shot and killed Gandhi. Gandhi's death was mourned not only in India, but all over the world.

India's first prime minister was Jawahar Lal Nehru, who had worked closely with Gandhi. People still remember the speech he made on the night India

From Many Into One 43

became free: "Long years ago we made a tryst [promise] with destiny, and now the time has come when we shall redeem our pledge. . . . A moment comes, which comes but rarely in history, when we step out from the old to the new, when an age ends, and when the soul of a nation suppressed finds utterance [a voice]."

On August 15, 1947, at the stroke of midnight, India entered a new part of its history—the age of independence. Proudly, India took its place among the free nations of the world.

An Independent Nation

The new government was faced with many problems, the biggest being India's fast-growing population. Many programs were started by the government to teach people to have smaller families. Even though the birth rate has slowed down, the population grows by fourteen million each year. Besides the new children, Indians are living longer today because of better health care. India's population has doubled since it became independent.

As you can imagine, providing education, employment, and food for so many people is not easy. In 1950 a planning commission was set up to make plans and set goals for five years at a time. India has gradually progressed from one five-year plan to the next.

After independence, India faced the tasks of becoming united and working out agreements with Pakistan. There were over 500 separate kingdoms within Indian borders. According to an agreement with the British, the ruler of each state would decide whether to join India or Pakistan. Sardar Patel, the deputy prime minister, persuaded most rulers to make their kingdoms a part of India. But the Hindu ruler of mostly-Muslim Kashmir also decided to join India. Because so many Muslims lived there, and because it was next to West Pakistan, Kashmir was wanted by Pakistan. Kashmir has been a source of trouble between India and Pakistan for many years.

Because it was new, India had some trouble with its neighbors in the 1960s and 1970s. In 1962 China attacked India over a border dispute. India suffered heavily at the hands of the Chinese. In 1965 fighting broke out between India and Pakistan. They had another war in 1971. This time, East Pakistan, which was over one thousand miles away from West Pakistan, became a separate country called Bangla Desh. During these conflicts, India realized that it had to be strong to protect itself. Money needed for other important projects had to be spent on making and buying war equipment.

Still, India wished to get along with its neighbors. Its leaders were very concerned about world peace. Nehru was shocked at the destruction caused by the Second World War. He was afraid that if smaller countries began to take sides with the two big powers, there would eventually be another big war that would destroy the world. He urged other nations to remain neutral and not to align themselves (take sides) with either the Soviet Union or the United States. Over ninety nations are members of the non-alignment movement today. India is friendly with both the United States and the Soviet Union.

Besides, India had so many big problems of its own, it needed help from any nation willing to help. India wanted friends, not enemies. The United States has been India's biggest friend and has helped in many different ways. For example, U.S. experts helped Indian farmers make the "Green Revolution." India no longer has to import food to feed its people; instead, its farmers can grow enough crops on their own.

The Soviet Union, Germany, and other European countries have helped with defense equipment and industry. Yet, compared to other young nations, India has borrowed little money from foreign banks. Though the country has received aid, India's achievements are largely its own.

Jawahar Lal Nehru (left) *and his daughter, Mrs. Indira Gandhi* (right) *have both led India as prime minister.*

An "Adventure in Democracy"

Independent India has been led by people who traveled, lived, and studied abroad. Gandhi, Nehru, and Mrs. Gandhi were all educated in the West. Many other Indians who trained abroad came back with new ideas and helped India go forward very quickly. One of these ideas was parliamentary democracy—the type of government where the people have power to make laws and elect officials. (India's villages have always had self-rule under their *panchayat*, or council of elders.)

It was not easy to apply this idea to India. Most democracies have a large, powerful, educated middle class. But in India, the majority of people were poor and uneducated. Many other poor nations have devel-

From Many Into One

oped into communist or military dictatorships. This means that a single person or a small group of people holds all the power. There, people have to do as they are told. Some feel that in a poor country this is a quick way to erase differences between rich and poor. India's leaders had visited many such countries. They did not want Indians to lose their freedom.

After centuries of foreign rule, many Indians felt that they could not rule themselves because they were too poor and unimportant. Would these people be able to choose their own leaders and make their own decisions? The world waited to see what would become of what Nehru called "India's adventure in democracy."

Nehru was the prime minister of India for seventeen years until his death in 1964. He was succeeded by Lal Bahadur Shastri, who died in office two years later. The new prime minister was Mrs. Indira Gandhi, Nehru's daughter. Mrs. Gandhi developed into a strong leader who guided India to victory in its war with Pakistan in 1971. After the fighting stopped, India had many other problems—rising prices, not enough food, and officials who committed crimes. Also, many Indian states wanted to do things their way instead of listening to the central government. Many people blamed Indira Gandhi for all of this.

In 1975, the Supreme Court said that Mrs. Gandhi had cheated during the last election and asked her to resign. Instead, she declared a "state of emergency" in the nation. Many people were put in jail. The press lost its freedom to print whatever it wanted. Indira Gandhi ruled with a strict hand for eighteen months. Some Indians felt that what the prime minister was doing was good for the country. Others were shocked by it. Many people felt this was the end of India's adventure in democracy.

But in January 1977, Mrs. Gandhi lifted the emergency and called for elections. Many Indians were angry with her for taking their freedoms away. They went to the polls and voted Mrs. Gandhi out of office. For the next two years, India was led by Prime Minister Morarji Desai. But things became worse in India. People began to feel that they were better off with Mrs. Gandhi after all. In 1980, they went to the polls and voted her back as prime minister. Almost 200 million people, 55 percent of the people who can vote, voted in that election. In the United States, also a democracy, 56 percent of voters usually go to the polls for an election. They showed the world that democracy could work in India.

This is the most exciting part of India's story—the change in her people. A few years of independence had shown the Indian people that they *could* rule

Nearly 55 percent of all Indians who could vote cast their ballots in the 1980 elections.

themselves, they *could* solve their problems. Earlier, when things went wrong, when monsoons or droughts destroyed their crops, Indian farmers would throw up their hands and say, "It is the will of God!" They felt they had no control over their lives. But the Green Revolution has taught Indian farmers that they *can* help themselves, they *can* make a difference. They can also have a say in how the country is run. Today, four out of ten MPs are farmers.

As a result of this new feeling of control and confidence, even poor Indians now make demands and expect to be listened to. But this "revolution of rising expectations" (as Mrs. Gandhi called it) is both good and bad. Many work hours are lost when workers go on strike to demand higher wages. Everyone wants more, and they don't want to wait for results.

For example, sometimes Indians feel very strongly about a situation. At times they take the law into their own hands to solve their problems. In 1983, Assamese Hindus and Muslim refugees from Bangla Desh fought. The Assamese were afraid of losing their majority to the Muslims who were coming into the state.

Also, in 1984 India had a shock when Indira Gandhi was assassinated. Earlier in the year, Sikh militants had fought with government troops in the Golden Temple in Amritsar over laws affecting Punjab. Sikh militants said that Mrs. Gandhi's shooting death by two of her guards was connected to the deaths in Amritsar. (Indira Gandhi's son Rajiv was made head of government after her assassination.)

Whatever the problem or crisis, Indians have pride in their country, pride in their heroes and their long story of 5,000 years. Most important of all, they know India's future is in their hands.

3. A Peaceful, Tolerant People

When one Indian meets another for the first time, he or she is likely to ask, "Which part of India are you from?" It is an important question, because, besides being Indian, he or she is also a Gujarati, Kashmiri, Tamil, or Punjabi. Because they have lived in their own regions for so many centuries, and traveled very little, if ever, in their lives, Indians from different states developed distinct customs and ways of doing things.

Often people try to guess where Indians are from just by looking at them. Most Indians have dark brown skin, black hair, and very dark brown eyes. However, people from different corners of the nation look quite unlike each other. Chances are that if a person is tall and fair-skinned, he or she is from the northern states of Kashmir or Punjab. But it is hard to tell, for sure; many light-skinned people also live in southern India. Hill folk and people from northeastern states such as Assam look Chinese or Burmese with their slanting eyes and pale skin. The people of the great northern plain resemble South Americans or Italians. You can see the differences clearly in the photos on the next pages.

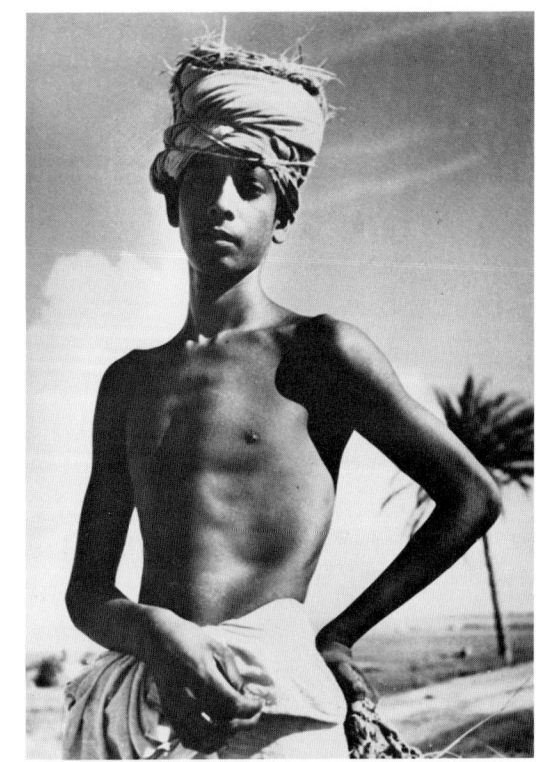

Courtesy of the Embassy of India

Photo © Stella Snead

These photos of Indian children show how very different the people from various corners of India can look.

Sometimes it is possible to guess where Indians are from by their last names. Names ending in *jee* (Bannerjee, Mukherjee) are usually Bengali names, while those ending in *kar* (Deolkar, Holkar) are generally Maharashtrian. Names ending in *wala* (Jhabwala, Sitarawala) are often Parsee names. People with Portuguese last names like *Braganza* and *DaCosta* are from Goa. *Patel*s are Gujaratis, *Rao*s are from southern India, and *Singh*s are either Rajputs or Punjabi Sikhs.

Different Peoples

The Punjabis, over whose fertile land came many invaders, became energetic, hard-working farmers and fighters. Used to constant change, Punjabis today are a progressive people, open to new ideas. Life in the states east of Punjab was more settled; there, people had time for the "finer things" in life. The people of Uttar Pradesh and Bihar, especially the Muslims, are known for their fine speech and manners. Bengalis also love poetry, literature, and the arts. Rabindranath Tagore, who won the 1907 Nobel Prize for Literature, was Bengali. Ravi Shankar, a world-famous musician, is also from Bengal.

Singer Lata Mangeshkar holds a world's record for taping over 25,000 songs for 1,800 movies in

A Peaceful, Tolerant People

twenty Indian languages. She is Maharashtrian and her people love music and drama. Maharashtra's neighbor Gujarat has many ports and a long history of trade. Therefore the Gujaratis are known as excellent traders and businesspeople. The most famous Gujarati was Mahatma Gandhi.

The people of southern India are known for their learning and culture (art, music, literature, etc.). "South Indians are very clever!" northerners will say. In Kerala, more people can read and write than in any other corner of India. Karnataka and Tamil Nadu have produced many brilliant scientists. C.V. Raman, who won the Nobel Prize for Physics in 1930, came from Tamil Nadu.

Different Dances

There are several kinds of dancing that have been performed for centuries. Tamil Nadu is the home of *Bharat Natyam*, a type of dancing 2,000 years old. Dancers in colorful silken costumes tell stories with their eyes and hands. They move their eyebrows up and down and their necks from side to side in a way that you would find hard to imitate. *Kathakali* dancers from Kerala act out stories about gods and ancient heroes. You can tell the different characters by the masklike makeup which is painted, layer by layer, onto their faces.

Some of the classical dances of India: Manipuri dancing (top); Kathakali dancers in their masklike makeup (above); a Bharat Natyam pose (right).

Courtesy of the Embassy of India

A Peaceful, Tolerant People

Manipuri dancers are slow and smooth in their movements. The women wear stiff, boxlike skirts, but the upper parts of their bodies sway gracefully. *Kathak* dancers of Uttar Pradesh move their feet in time to small drums called *tablas*. Like most Indian dancers, they wear rows and rows of little bells around their ankles. Dressed in rich satin clothes, Kathak dancers used to perform in the courts of long-ago Mughal kings.

Today, Indian children take lessons in Bharat Natyam and Kathak after school, just as American children learn ballet and piano. Some children learn to play the tabla, and others learn the *sitar*, a long-stringed instrument. Classical music and dancing take years of training and practice, but children love to perform in front of an audience, dressed up in colorful costumes.

Different Dress

Every Indian state has clothing of its own, so on an Indian street today, you can see costumes of all kinds. In the cities, most middle-class men wear Western clothes to work. At home, northern men wear loose cotton pajamalike pants and knee-length shirts. In the fields, farmers drape a white piece of fabric called a *dhoti* around their waists and between their legs. Because of the heat, they often stay bare-chested. Southern men wear brightly colored clothes called *lungis* around their waists. Many Indian men wear some sort of turban on their heads.

Rajasthani women dress in colorful ankle-length skirts that swirl and sway as they walk. Punjabi women wear baggy pants with a knee-length shirt called a *kameez*. Across their shoulders they wear a long scarf. Sometimes the pants are tightly fitted and gathered at the ankle. These are called *churidar pajamas* and can be worn with long shirts by men or women.

Usually, though, most Indian women wear some form of the *sari*. This is six yards of fabric draped around the waist and over the shoulder. Tall or short, thin or fat, any woman can adjust the sari to her size by making a few more or less tucks or folds. It is a very easy-to-wear garment and can be made of any material—cotton, silk, or nylon. Fabric from France is very popular with the wealthy. Women who follow fashion love to buy saris made in America and Japan.

Indian women take pride in their thick, long hair, which they coil into buns on their heads. Girls usually have long, shiny braids, which sometimes fall below their waists. However, city girls often cut their hair short like American girls. Modern teenagers like to wear Western clothes, especially jeans imported from America. (They usually wear more traditional clothes to school and college.)

Girls often put a little round dot called a *bindi* in the middle of their foreheads. A bindi can be of any color. Women sometimes wear bindis to match their clothes. Indian clothes are usually very colorful because Indians love bright colors.

Colors also have meaning for Indians. White is the color of sadness and mourning; widows wear white. Red is the color for joy; brides usually wear a shade of red. Brides and married women use red bindis. They may also put a little red powder called *sindoor* in the parting of their hair. In villages, and in old-fashioned families, married women keep their heads and sometimes even their faces covered in front of strangers. This custom is called *purdah*.

In ancient India, women did not have to cover their faces and had a good deal of freedom. However, when invaders started sweeping through the northern plains, women had to be protected. They began staying indoors and gradually began to lose their freedom. They almost never appeared in public. The south, however, had fewer invasions, and women did not have to hide. Today, the Indian constitution gives women all over the nation the very same rights as men, including the right to vote.

Indian people are very fond of bright colors.

Indian Ways and Customs

However modern they may be, Indians still like to keep their Indian ways. When greeting each other, Indians do not shake hands. Instead, they fold their palms together and say "Namaste," which is Sanskrit for "I bow my head to you." Indians also often touch the feet of older relatives when meeting or parting.

Older people are greatly respected in Indian society. The longer you live, the more experienced and wise you must be, Indians feel, so they always seek the advice of their elders in important matters. Old peo-

A Peaceful, Tolerant People

ple do not bother to hide their age. "My hair did not grow white in the sun," elders remind young people. White hair is a symbol of age and wisdom and is considered worthy of respect.

Children are taught to respect and obey their elders from the very beginning. To be polite, the word *ji* is added to the name of an older person. All adults are "Aunty ji" or "Uncle ji" even if they are not related. An Indian child would be thought rude if he or she called a neighbor "Mr. Brown." It would have to be "Uncle Brown."

Indians regard the whole world as family. Gandhi ji was called *Bapu* (father) by many. India's first prime minister was known as *Chacha* (Uncle) Nehru. Even on the street, strangers address each other as "Father," "Mother," "Brother," or "Sister." Children are called "Son" or "Daughter."

Children are considered a gift from God to be held, hugged, loved, and spoiled for as long as possible. In well-to-do homes, childhood is a time for play and no worries. Children do no work except school work. Unlike American children, they do not get jobs baby-sitting, cutting grass, or delivering newspapers. In India, there are too many poor adults without jobs who can do such work.

However, children from poor homes are expected to help their parents from the day they are able. Older children take care of their younger brothers and sisters. Some work along with their parents. Poor families often have many children and struggle hard to get enough to eat. They own few clothes and no toys, and live in small huts with little space to themselves.

While people are gradually expecting more out of life in India, even the very poor are content with very little. They accept their hard lives with good cheer. Laborers sing at the end of a long, hot day's work. Hindu writings warn against too much wealth. They teach people not to get too attached to worldly things. Just do your duty and leave the rest to God and fate.

Rich or poor, many Indians believe their fate or *kismet* is already decided when they are born. They are very interested in knowing what the future holds for them. When a child is born, his or her parents may call in an astrologer to prepare a *Janam Patri* (horoscope or birth chart). Astrologers claim they can predict a person's future by studying the pattern of stars under which he or she was born: when he will marry, how many children she will have, whether the children will be boys or girls.

Indians especially want their children to be boys. "May you have many sons!" is a common blessing for young women. When a son is born or married, sweets called *laddoos* are given out to relatives. A bite of something sweet is thought to be lucky. Indians

A Peaceful, Tolerant People

sweeten their mouths with a piece of laddoo or even a few grains of sugar before an exam, during a ceremony, or on a happy occasion. Nobody understands the reasons for some of these old customs, but they follow them anyway, because customs and traditions are very important to the Indian people.

Indians take pride in being simple and down to earth. Appearances are not important; what is beneath the surface counts, Indians feel. They do not spend a lot of time making things appear better than they are. Instead, modesty is very important to Indians. Adults are careful not to boast about themselves. Even very wealthy or intelligent people talk about themselves as though they are poor or not at all clever. Yet, parents cannot help showing off their children. A child may be asked to sing a song or recite a poem when visitors drop by.

Good Indian Neighbors

Indian families are used to visitors just dropping by. Because hospitality is an important tradition, even unexpected guests who show up at a bad time are welcomed warmly and treated with respect. Since most homes do not have telephones, people just take a chance and drop by if they wish to see someone. In any case, being on time or doing things as planned are just not very important.

Hurry and haste seem rude and senseless to Indians, who prefer to be easy-going and casual. "Please do not be formal," guests will say to their hosts.

Unlike American mothers, Indian women do not usually keep calendars to plan activities. Things just happen. When someone is late or plans do not work out, people will shrug and say, "Never mind" or "Let it be." People are more important than plans.

Indians are used to being around other people. Someone is always coming or going in an Indian home, if only peddlers stopping by to sell their goods. Life is seldom lonely in India. But then, since living conditions are often crowded, people cannot keep too many secrets from each other. Everybody knows everybody else's business. People often ask each other personal questions the first time they meet. "How old are you?" and "How many children do you have?" are favorite questions.

Indians are involved in each other's lives because they depend on each other for help and support. People in sorrow and sickness are never left alone. In the hospital, patients always have a family member staying in their rooms to look after them. At funerals people embrace each other and weep and wail openly. Indians are a warm, affectionate people, and they are not afraid to express their emotions. No matter which language they speak, you can tell what they feel because they use their hands and faces freely.

Worship As a Way of Life

Religion is a central part of Indian life. Temples, churches, and *mosques* (Muslim temples) can be found in every city. Because they have lived side by side for so many centuries, people of different religions have borrowed many customs and habits from each other. It becomes hard to say which custom is Hindu, Muslim, Sikh, or Indian. Whatever their religion, most Indians cover their heads and take off their shoes before they enter a place of worship.

Worship is a way of thinking and living in India. Indians are always prepared to pray, to bow their heads in humbleness and thankfulness. Farmers put flowers on their bullocks and tractors. Craftworkers burn incense in front of their tools. Hindus see God in everything, so, for them, many things are sacred—trees, rivers, and even cows.

Hindus believe in rebirth or reincarnation—that is, when people die, their souls are reborn as something or someone else. Their deeds, or *karma*, in life determine whether that rebirth will be as, say, a

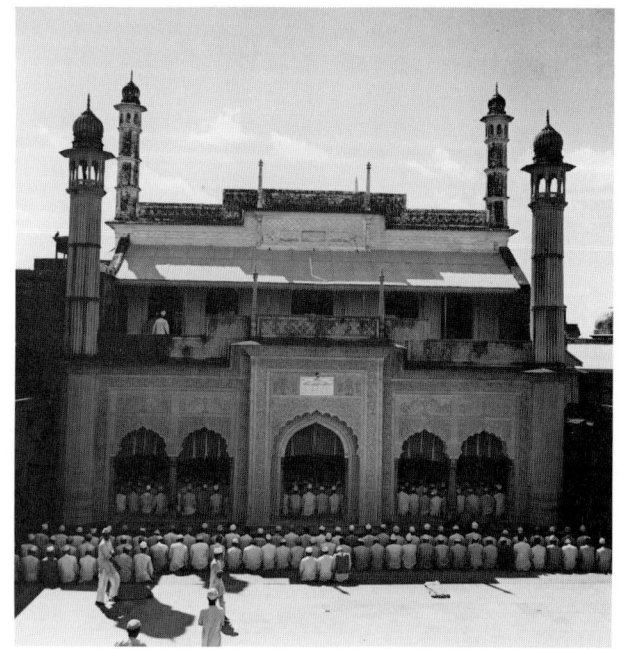

Beautiful temples are everywhere in India. To the right, Muslims worship at a mosque; below is a Hindu temple in Madhya Pradesh.

Courtesy of the Embassy of India

A Peaceful, Tolerant People

worm, a dog, or a human. Karma also determines whether the next life will be happy or sad. When things go wrong for Hindus, they can blame their karma in their last birth. To have a better birth next time, they must do good deeds in their present life.

Hindus do not have a holy day in the week as do Christians, Jews, and Muslims. While some families visit a temple daily, others seldom do. Many families have shrines called *puja* rooms in their own homes, and they worship there every morning. Some families keep statues of their favorite gods and goddesses which they wash and dress often.

Hindus worship God in many forms. Worship is so personal that every member of the family may pray to a different god. Although there are some Hindus who are against the caste system and praying to statues, and who believe in only one God, most Hindus worship Shiva, or Rama, or Krishna or Durga.

Muslims do not have a caste system as Hindus do. Their God is *Allah* and their holy book is called the *Koran*. Muslims pray in their mosques on Fridays and pray five times a day for the rest of the week. Many Muslims are fine artists and craftworkers. Quite a few famous Indian musicians are Muslims.

Sikhism brought many ideas from Hinduism and Islam together. Sikhs also do not have a caste system and believe in equality among people. Sikhs follow the teachings of their ten *gurus* (teachers), the first of whom was Guru Nanak.

Sikhs worship in temples called *gurudwaras*, the main one being the Golden Temple in Amritsar. Their holy book, the *Guru Granth Sahib*, contains the teachings of the ten gurus. Many Punjabi Hindus also visit gurudwaras regularly and study the *Granth Sahib* in their homes. The Sikhs, who are a little over half the Punjabi population, are only 2 percent of the Indian population (but an important part of the Indian army).

Another small but important minority are the Zoroastrians or Parsees, the followers of an ancient prophet called Zarathustra. Wealthy Parsee manufacturers have done much for India by building factories, schools, and hospitals. Fire is sacred to the Zoroastrians, and they worship in Fire Temples. Their God is *Ahura Mazda* and their holy book is the *Zend Avesta*.

Although Buddhism started in India and spread to other countries, few Buddhists are left in India. However, the Indian philosophy of *ahimsa* or nonviolence was preached by the Buddha (as well as by Mahavira) who taught kindness to all living things. Today Buddhists, as well as many Hindus, do not eat meat, because they are against killing animals for food. The Jains, another religious group, are so strict about this that some wear cloth masks over their mouths. That way, they do not breathe in and kill the tiny insects in the air.

Alike and Different

Gandhi, who was greatly influenced by Jain thought, made nonviolence famous throughout the world during India's freedom struggle. By and large, Indians are a peaceful, nonviolent, tolerant people. They live and let live. Even the police do not carry guns. But now and then, newspapers report about Indians of different religions fighting and killing each other. Outsiders begin to wonder how long people of so many different languages and religions can live together in one nation.

But while differences divide and separate Indians, they also combine and connect them. Every Indian belongs to several groups based on language, religion, region, and economic status. Although Hindus from Andhra Pradesh and Uttar Pradesh have many differences, they have their religion in common. Although Punjabi Hindus may vary somewhat from Punjabi Sikhs, they share the language, food, and costume of the Punjab. Although a Hindu from Tamil Nadu may be quite unlike a Kashmiri Muslim, they may have a lot in common because they speak English and read the same national newspapers. The people of India are so interlinked by their differences and their similarities that it is difficult to separate one group entirely from the other.

Whether they are Hindu or Muslim, Kashmiri or Gujarati, rich or poor, all Indians share certain values. Love of family, respect for elders, hospitality and humbleness, tolerance and tradition, warmth and welcome—all these make up the "Indian-ness" of an Indian.

4. Holy Books and Witty Fables

Indians have stories and fables about everything, and most of their stories are about gods because there are so many, many gods in India. Educated Hindus know that there is only one God—One only, without second. God is the Self, *Brahman*, *Atman*, the human soul. God is everywhere, from the lowliest mud hut to magnificent temples, and is in everything, larger than the universe, smaller than a mustard seed.

But simple folk need an easier God to love—one they can see and understand. So their gods each take many forms; they look and live like them, get married, and have children. Their gods have feelings: like humans they love, hate, get angry, and quarrel with each other. But they have superhuman powers too; they grant wishes and give protection. And humans have always needed protection from the powers of Nature, from things more powerful than they. So they pray out of fear and love and in thankfulness to the gods who they believe have control over the universe.

This is why the Aryans worshipped Surya, the Sun; Soma, the Moon; Varuna, the Ocean; Indra, the god of Storms; and Agni, the god of Fire. But after they had lived in India for some time, the Aryans began to pray to other gods.

Three Hindu Gods

In Hindu myths, there are three main gods, who created or who run the earth. They are *Brahma*, the creator; *Shiva*, the destroyer; and *Vishnu*, the preserver. Each of these gods controls parts of life, and with each function the god is given a different name.

Brahma is called by many names. He created the world. Although Brahma was very important to early Hindu myths, he is not much worshipped today.

Many people do pray to Shiva, however. Shiva has many names and many forms. Sometimes he is Natraja, the Lord of Dance. Statues of Natraja show him dancing on the body of a demon who is a dwarf. Sometimes Shiva is called Pasupati, the Lord of the Animals. At other times he sits cross-legged on top of snowy Mount Kailash in the Himalayas, meditating (thinking deep thoughts). His body is covered with ashes, snakes wind around him, and his hair is wild.

Shiva's "Family"

Many temples have been built for Shiva, for he is powerful and people are afraid of him. Even his wife,

A statue of Natraja, the Lord of Dance (another name for Shiva).

Devi, can be frightening. Sometimes she is Kali, a dark, angry goddess with many arms. She is also Durga, goddess of war and weapons, always fighting evil demons. At other times she is Parvati, gentle wife and mother of four—Skanda, Lakshmi, Saraswati, and Ganesh.

Ganesh's head was accidentally cut off as a child. In his panic, Shiva replaced it with the first one he found—an elephant's head. Ganesh is a roly-poly, good-natured god. He loves to eat; his worshippers bring him lots of fruit. He has many followers, because he is the god of wisdom and success. People pray to him before they begin any important project.

Ganesh's sister, the fair and lovely Saraswati, is married to Brahma the Creator. In one hand she holds a *veena* (a musical instrument) and in the other a book. She is the goddess of sixty-four arts and sciences. It is said that she invented Sanskrit and that the Vedas, the earliest Aryan hymns, sprang from her head. As the goddess of learning and the arts, she is a favorite with scholars, artists, and musicians.

Lakshmi is everyone's favorite goddess, for she is the goddess of wealth and good fortune. A first-born daughter is considered a Lakshmi and very lucky. Usually Lakshmi sits on a lotus, but sometimes she rides the *garuda*, the man-vulture, with her husband Vishnu, the preserver of the world.

Vishnu and His Avatars

Vishnu, the preserver, the god of life, is worshipped in love, not in fear as Shiva is. Hindu myths say that Vishnu sleeps on top of Ananta, the serpent

Hindus worship many gods and like to have statues or pictures of them. Above are images of Ganesh, the elephant-headed god, and Lakshmi, the goddess of good fortune.

(snake) of Eternity. When the world is in danger, Vishnu awakes, takes the form of a human or an animal, and comes to earth to save it. Each person he becomes is called an *avatar* of Vishnu.

Hindus believe Vishnu has come to earth nine times. One of the most loved, popular appearances of

Vishnu is *Rama*, the seventh avatar of the god. Rama was born as a prince. The story of Rama's life, the *Ramayana*, is one of the holy books of the Hindus. Besides being an exciting story, the *Ramayana* also shows how a perfect Hindu should act.

The Story of Rama

Once, long ago, a mighty king called Dasrath lived in Ayodhya, the capital of his rich, powerful kingdom on the north Indian plain. Dasrath had three wives and four sons, named Rama, Lakshman, Bharat, and Shatrugan. He was proud of all four, but his favorite son was the eldest—Rama.

Rama was tall and handsome and good with all kinds of weapons, especially the bow and arrow. He was loved by the people of Ayodhya for his kind and noble nature. It was no surprise to his people when Dasrath announced that he wished to appoint Rama the next king.

But Kaikeyi, Dasrath's third queen, objected. She wanted her own son, Bharat, to be crown prince. Once, long before, Dasrath agreed to give Kaikeyi two wishes, but Kaikeyi had never asked for anything. Now she went to Dasrath and demanded that he grant the wishes he had promised her.

Holy Books and Witty Fables

She wished for Dasrath to appoint Bharat crown prince and for him to send away (exile) Rama from Ayodhya for fourteen years. Dasrath begged her to change her mind. But Kaikeyi remained firm. A prince can never go back on his promise. Dasrath sadly had to do as she asked.

Rama accepted his father's command to leave quietly, with bowed head and joined palms. It was a son's duty to respect and obey his parents without argument. Rama got ready to leave for the forest. His lovely wife Sita went with him. Loyal Lakshman, Rama's favorite brother, also followed Rama.

All Ayodhya wept when they left. Soon King Dasrath died in sorrow. Bharat, who had been away, returned. He was angry with his mother Kaikeyi when he learned what had happened. He ran after Rama and begged him to return and rule Ayodhya. But Rama had promised his father and would not come back. Sadly Bharat went home, taking Rama's sandals with him, which he placed on the throne. For fourteen years he sat beside the throne waiting for Rama's exile to end.

Rama, Sita, and Lakshman wandered south through thick forests, living on nuts, berries, and animals they hunted. One day Surupnaka, a female demon, visited them in their hut. She had an argument with Lakshman, who, in a fit of temper, cut her ears and nose with a sword. Howling, Surupnaka fled to her brother Raavan, the ten-headed demon king of Lanka (Ceylon). Angered by his sister's story, Raavan decided to punish the two brothers by stealing the lovely Sita.

With the help of a magical golden deer, Raavan drew Rama deep into the forest. Soon Lakshman became worried and went in search of Rama. Now that there was no one to protect Sita, Raavan grabbed her and flew away with her in his winged chariot to Lanka.

Finding Sita gone, Rama was furious. He asked for help from Hanuman, a monkey general. Now, Hanuman was no ordinary monkey. He was the son of the Wind and could fly like a bird. He flew across the ocean to Lanka and found Sita sitting sadly in Raavan's garden (for she refused to live in his palace with him). Hanuman dropped Rama's ring in Sita's lap and told her help was on the way.

Rama and Lakshman, with the help of all the animals in the forest, built a bridge across the ocean to Lanka. Even the little squirrel wanted to help, but all the other animals laughed at him. Rama lovingly stroked the squirrel's back. That is why, it is said, the Indian squirrel has three white stripes on its back.

When Rama got to Lanka, he attacked Raavan. Finally, Raavan was killed and Sita was rescued from

An illustration from a four-hundred-year-old translation of the Ramayana, *showing Rama killing Raavan.*

Lanka. The fourteen years of exile were then over; Rama, Sita, and Lakshman returned to a joyful Ayodhya, where Rama ruled for many happy years.

The *Ramayana* was written by a holy man named Valmiki. Today, Rama is yet another name for God.

When villagers greet each other they say, "Ram-Ram." When people go over their prayer beads they mutter his name. Every Hindu wants a son as obedient as Rama, a brother as loyal as Lakshman, and a wife as devoted as Sita.

Krishna

Even more widely worshipped than Rama is Krishna, the eighth avatar of Vishnu. Krishna was born so that the people of Mathura would be freed from an evil king, Kansa. A story said that the eighth son of Devaki, Kansa's cousin, would kill Kansa. Hearing this story, Kansa imprisoned Devaki and her husband Vasudeva.

Krishna, Devaki's eighth baby, was born while the couple was in prison. Vasudeva stole out with him in the middle of the night; by some miracle, the prison guards were asleep. Vasudeva had no trouble crossing the river to the town of Gokul, where his friend Nand the cowherd lived. Nand's wife Yashoda had just had a baby girl. Quietly, Vasudeva switched the two babies and carried the girl back to prison with him. The next day, Kansa tried to kill the baby, thinking she was Devaki's eighth child. But the girl flew out of his hands and turned into lightning, saying "Your destroyer still lives, Kansa!"

Yashoda and Nand brought Krishna up as if he were their own son. Krishna was a mischievous, lovable boy who was always playing jokes. He turned over the milk pails of the *gopis* (milk maids) and stole butter from his mother's kitchen. But even as a child he performed miracles. Once he fought a many-headed snake who was poisoning the river Jamuna. He defeated it by dancing on its heads, forcing it to leave the river. Another time, Krishna saved Gokul from being flooded by a terrible storm. He picked up the mountain Govardhan and held it over the town like an umbrella until the rain stopped.

Krishna was a hero to the people of Gokul, but he was especially adored by the *gopis*. One gopi named Radha was Krishna's favorite. Today, Radha is a popular name for Indian girls. Krishna is lovingly called different names by his many worshippers. To some he is Shyam (evening), for he is blue, the color of twilight. To others he is Gopal—cowherd. Many know him as Nandlal, son of Nand. Usually he holds a flute to his smiling lips as he plays for the delight of cows and gopis alike.

Krishna grew up and killed Kansa, the task for which he was born. But he is remembered most for his role in the *Mahabharata*. This, like the *Ramayana*, is a Hindu epic: with 100,000 verses, the *Mahabharata* is the world's longest poem.

A Tale from the Mahabharata

Ancient India was once ruled by a blind king called Dhritarashtra. He had one hundred sons called the Kauravas. He also raised his dead brother's five sons, the Pandavas. Both groups would someday rule their kingdom. All the boys were taught fighting skills by Dronacharya, a great teacher. But the best in archery and the arts of war was Arjuna, the third Pandava.

Now the oldest Kaurava was jealous of his cousins, the Pandavas, and wanted somehow to take their share of the kingdom for himself. He challenged the oldest Pandava to a game of dice. The Kaurava used trick dice; the Pandava brother soon lost everything he possessed to the Kauravas.

The Pandavas were exiled. They had to leave the kingdom for thirteen years. But after the exile was over, the Kauravas refused to give the five Pandavas their share of the kingdom. The Kauravas and the Pandavas went to war. Both groups asked for help from Lord Krishna. Krishna offered them a choice: a huge army or himself, unarmed. The Kauravas chose the army, and Arjuna asked Krishna to be his chariot driver.

Just before the battle, Arjuna had second thoughts about trying to kill his cousins. Krishna explained to

Students of the India School in Maryland act out the story of Rama.

Arjuna that it was a warrior's duty to fight for justice, and that he should remove all doubts from his mind. Krishna's talk to Arjuna is called the *Bhagavad Gita*, another important holy book of Hindus today.

After a long, hard battle, the Pandavas won back their throne. Yudhishtra, the eldest Pandava, ruled for many happy years.

Folktales

As in many other countries, India also has its share of folktales and fairy stories. According to legend, there was a king who thought his three sons would never learn anything of value. Then, one day, an old man appeared in his court and offered to teach the princes common sense and wisdom in six months. His offer was gladly accepted. The old man told the boys many stories about birds, animals, and men. Each story taught a lesson. These wise and witty little fables were collected into a large book called the *Panchatantra*. They were later translated into European languages. Here is a story from that book.

One day a jackal accidentally fell into a pot of dye and turned blue. When he climbed out and returned to the forest, no one knew him. In fact, the other creatures ran away from him in fear. They had never before seen a blue animal!

The jackal was quick to make the best of the situation. He told the animals not to be afraid. He said that God had sent him there to be their king. For a long time the animals believed him. They treated him like a king and brought him many things to eat.

One night, the jackal heard a pack of jackals howling in the distance. All this time, he had missed his old friends and old ways. Forgetting he was king, he threw back his head and sent an answering howl. Immediately, the other animals realized he was only a jackal. Angry at being tricked, they chased him out of the forest.

Moral: You cannot fool all the people all the time!

5. Sweets, Ceremonies, and Celebrations

Rows and rows of flickering flames light a dark Indian night in November. In northern India, Hindu homes have been lit with lamps. Even the president's palace in New Delhi is draped with thousands of lightbulbs. It is *Diwali*, festival of lights, a time all over India for worship and celebration.

On this day, Hindus celebrate Rama's return after his years of exile. It is also a day to worship Lakshmi, the goddess of good fortune. Business owners start new business records. For them, Diwali is the beginning of a new year.

During Diwali, people exchange greeting cards and gifts of sweets. Shops are filled with mouth-watering mountains of treats. Rows of pink coconut *barfi* (toffee) stand next to stacks of green pistachio barfi, which are next to mounds of golden yellow *laddoos* (sweet balls). Every piece is covered with a film of fine silver foil that can be eaten.

The day of Diwali is spent decorating homes with colorful floor patterns done in colored powder. Hundreds of little oil-filled lamps are placed in rows along walls and window ledges (in Sanskrit, Diwali means "rows of lamps.") When darkness falls, they will be

Photo © Stella Snead

Buildings have been lined with lights for Diwali and other holidays for many years.

lit, one by one, to light the way for Lakshmi and to welcome her at each home.

After Lakshmi *puja* (ceremony or worship), everyone prepares for some fun with firecrackers. Little children are both frightened and excited as they hold sizzling sparklers. They place their hands over their ears when the bombs boom, and jump up and down for joy when fountains of colorful sparks shoot up

Sweets, Ceremonies, and Celebrations

into the sky. The merry-making continues until late. Many adults stay awake all night, playing cards or keeping a lamp lit before Lakshmi's statue so that it does not die out before the sun rises.

The next morning is an ordinary day; children go unwillingly back to school. But they won't have long to wait before another festival comes along. With so many religions and so many gods, there is no lack of holy days or holidays on the Indian calendar. Every major faith is honored by at least one official holiday.

Some Religious Holidays

Christmas is a nationwide holiday, although it is celebrated only by Christians. An Indian Christmas is quite different from what we are used to in America. Except in churches and schools, there are usually no Christmas trees, Christmas stockings, or Santa Claus. Even the hymns sound different because they are often sung in regional dialects. In Goa, which is mostly Christian, Christmas is a time for widespread merry-making. But for most Indian Christians, it is a time for prayer and remembering Christ.

Buddha is remembered on *Buddha Purnima*, celebrated on a full-moon day in May. Buddha preached kindness to animals, so his followers buy caged birds and set them free. They also pay butchers to free animals ready to be killed and eaten. Buddha Purnima is the day Buddha reached wisdom under the bodhi tree. It is also the day he died and the day he was born. *Mahavir Jayanti*, the birthday of the Jain saint, and *Gandhi Jayanti* are also national holidays.

The birthday of Guru Nanak, the founder of Sikhism, is also a government holiday. On this day, *gurudwaras* (Sikh temples) are crowded with worshippers. At the end of the services, a huge meal is served. All are welcome to this free feast which is prepared by volunteers. Sikhs believe in service and cooperation. Even little children help perform odd jobs around the temple.

Schools and offices are closed all over India on *Id-ul-Fitr*, a Muslim holy day. This day marks the end of *Ramadan*, which is a whole month of fasting from dawn until sundown. With real rejoicing the new moon is sighted, for it signals three days of feasting and fun. The exact dates of Ramadan change every year. This is because Muslims use a lunar calendar in which every month consists of twenty-nine and a half days. Since the lunar year is eleven days shorter than our solar calendar, the Muslim year is shorter than ours by eleven days every year.

The Hindu calendar also goes by the cycles of the moon, but in order to catch up with the solar year, astrologers add an extra month every three years.

Quite confusing, isn't it? To make matters worse, the astrologers sometimes disagree on how to add the additional month. In 1982, India had two Diwalis!

Merry Festivals

Diwali is a religious festival, but people find many other reasons to celebrate. The changing of the seasons and the reaping of the harvest are good excuses to rejoice. India has two harvests every year. One is in April or May, the other in January.

In mid-January, Tamil Nadu storehouses overflow with newly harvested rice and sugar cane. *Pongalo* means "to overflow," and *Pongal* is the name of a three-day harvest festival, as well as a special food. "Pongalo pongal!" the women call to each other as the pongal, a dish made of rice, brown sugar, and milk, boils and overflows the pot. The women have scrubbed and cleaned their homes. They also wash and decorate their cattle. The women feed the cattle specially because they are grateful for their help all year in the fields. They thank the sun for ripening their crops. Indra, god of thunder and seasons, is praised by the thunderous beating of drums

In the state of Punjab, bands of children go from home to home chanting rhymes and begging for cow dung cakes and bits of firewood for a *Lohri* bonfire. During Lohri, Punjabis thank the sun for heating them through the winter cold by lighting a huge fire at night.

Soon after Lohri comes *Basant*, the first day of spring, a day to fly kites. Basant is a "yellow" day. February fields are covered with yellow mustard blooms. Everyone wears yellow clothes and eats yellow sweet rice.

But a day of many colors is *Holi*, a March spring festival. Some say that Hollika, an ogre who devoured children, was killed and burned this day. Some connect this day with Krishna teasing the cow herds. Whatever the origin, Holi is a fun-filled day of mischief.

During Holi, children play pranks that they would not otherwise get away with. For several days before Holi, they fling water-filled balloons on well-dressed passers-by. Giggling, the children run out of sight before they can be caught.

On the day of Holi no one wears clothes he or she cares about. About midmorning, neighbors and relatives start calling on each other. They carry buckets of colored water and packages of brightly colored powders. Gleefully, they rub the colors on each other. Shrieking in excitement, they chase back and forth, shooting jets of colored water at each other. After

Photo © Stella Snead

The colored powders with which people smear each other on Holi are sold in bazaars.

hours of play, these multicolored people head home to wash the colors off their hair and bodies. For many days they will laugh about their adventures on this funny spring festival.

New Years in Spring

Navroze is a spring festival celebrated by the Parsees on March 21. Freshly cleaned homes are decorated with fragrant flowers and colorful floor designs. Families sit down to a large feast after services in the Fire Temple. Parsees are fire worshippers who fled from Persia 1,200 years ago to India, where they have always been free to practice their religion, Zoroastrianism. For some Parsees, Navroze is a day of thanksgiving; for others, it is their new year.

Punjabi Hindus celebrate New Year on *Baisakhi*, which is a full-moon day in April/May. It is at the same time as the wheat harvest in Punjab. Gaily dressed Punjabis go to a Baisakhi *Mela* (fair), where they sing, dance, ride ferris wheels, and generally have fun. Adults and children all over India look forward to *melas*, which are held for various reasons throughout the year.

Holy Journeys

The mela of all melas is the *Kumbh Mela* held at Allahabad every twelve years. Allahabad is the holiest of these places since it is at the joining of the Ganges and Jamuna rivers. Hindus believe that bathing in the Ganges washes away their

Sweets, Ceremonies, and Celebrations

sins and protects them from evil. Pilgrims carry back the sacred Ganges water in bottles as a souvenir. Though visitors bathe in the Ganges every day, the Kumbh Mela attracts ten million pilgrims!

People make pilgrimages at times other than holidays, too. Over ten thousand people visit the Venkateshwara temple in Andhra Pradesh every day. They bring gifts of cloth and money, making this the richest temple in India. They also cut off and offer their hair to Lord Vishnu, to whom this temple is dedicated.

No matter which god they honor, most large temples have an annual procession through the city. One of the most famous temple processions is held at the Jagannath temple in Puri in Orissa state. *Jagannath* is another name for Krishna; every year in Puri his statue is taken for a ride on a huge chariot. The chariot is forty-five feet high, and each of its sixteen wheels is seven feet in width. Images of Krishna's brothers and sisters follow on smaller chariots. Four thousand people are needed just to pull the large chariot along. Many hundreds of thousands gather to witness this ceremony every summer.

Birthdays and Boat Races

Towards the end of August, *Janam Ashtami*, Krishna's birthday, is celebrated all over India. It is

Millions of people come to Allahabad for the Kumbh Mela, where they bathe in the holy Ganges River.

cause for special festivity in Krishna's birthplace, Mathura. An image of the baby Krishna is placed in a cradle and draped with ropes of flowers. Towards nightfall, people gather at the temple to hear the story of Krishna's birth. Then, at midnight, amid great rejoicing, dancing, and clanging of temple bells, Krishna is born. Adults break their day-long fast and eat the numerous dishes that have been prepared for the occasion.

Sweets, Ceremonies, and Celebrations

Many religious festivals begin with fasting and end with feasting after prayers. Before prayers, an offering of *halwa* (a sweet cereal) or some other sweet is placed before a shrine. After prayers, it is considered blessed by the gods and is distributed among those present. In the state of Maharashtra, *panchamrit*, made from milk, yoghurt, butter, honey and sugar, is a common offering.

On Krishna's birthday, an earthenware pot that holds panchamrit and money is hung over the street. Children form a pyramid by climbing on each other's shoulders to reach and break the pot. This is how little Krishna used to steal butter from his mother's kitchen, no matter how high up she placed it.

In September, Maharashtrians celebrate another favorite festival, *Ganesh Chaturthi*, dedicated to Ganesh, the elephant-headed god of wisdom. The Maharashtrians, who are a theater-loving, artistic people, hold drama competitions for nine days in Ganesh's honor.

Also in late summer, the people of the southwest state of Kerala celebrate *Onam*, a ten-day festival dedicated to King Mahabali, an ancient ruler. Round clay pyramids, representing Mahabali and Vishnu, sit in every freshly cleaned home. A new row of flowers is placed around the pyramids every day, until by the tenth day they are completely covered with flowers.

A rainy Independence Day in New Delhi.

Since Kerala is a state of streams and canals, the people of Kerala are excellent sailors. Sports and boat races are a highlight of Onam.

Although some holidays are regional, January 26, India's Republic Day, is a holiday for the whole nation. New Delhi is the site of the impressive Republic Day Parade. Soldiers march and bands play. School children perform dances and exercises to the cheers and applause of the watching crowds. Colorful floats representing each state move past the president of India who sits in the grandstand.

The prime minister stands on the walls of the Red Fort in Delhi and addresses a large crowd on August 15 every year. This is the day India became independent from British rule—the "birthday" of India. Since August is a monsoon month, people often get very wet if they haven't brought their umbrellas!

Good Over Evil

Soon after the monsoons, Hindus all over India start preparing for *Dassera*, a major ten-day festival. Every region has a different manner and reason for celebrating Dassera. But it is always a celebration of the victory of good over evil.

In Bengal, Dassera is known as *Durga Puja.* Bengali children get new clothes during puja holidays. They go every day with their parents to the worship service organized by the neighborhood. Durga, the mother goddess, sits on her lion surrounded by her four children—Ganesh and his rat, Skanda on his peacock, Lakshmi on her lotus, and Saraswati on her white swan.

Bengalis worship Saraswati in the spring, but other places in India have Saraswati Puja during Dassera. Artists, musicians, and scholars place their books, instruments, and tools of their crafts in front of the goddess of learning. They pray that, like her, they may be intelligent and skillful in what they do.

In Karnataka state, Dassera is the time for honoring Durga with a magnificent parade. Dassera also marks the doll festival of Karnataka. Rows of dolls and figures of gods, animals, and humans are displayed on a stairlike platform. Children look forward to taking out the dolls they put away the year before and adding other dolls to their collections.

In northern India, Dassera represents the battle of Rama with Raavan. Every year the story of the *Ramayana* is either retold by a priest or acted out by actors. This is called the *Ramleela*, and is presented for a couple of hours every day during Dassera. In Delhi, a special area set aside for this is called the Ramleela grounds.

At the Ramleela grounds, three huge figures, 120 to 150 feet high, are built. These represent Raavan, the demon king, and his two giant brothers. The figures are stuffed with firecrackers. On the tenth day of Dassera a flaming arrow (from Rama's bow) sets Raavan on fire. As the crowds cheer, Raavan and his brothers explode and burn to ashes.

Gaily the crowds go home. Good has triumphed over Evil again. Dassera is over for another year. In a few days it will be Diwali. Thus, the cycle of worship and celebration continues, year after year.

6. Families, Homes, and Foods

In an Indian family, relatives are so important that each relationship has a separate name. For an Indian boy, his mother's brother would be his *Mama* and his father's brother would be his *Chacha*. It is not enough to be related; *how* you are related is very important, because you behave in a certain way with every role and relationship.

For instance, brothers and sisters have a very special relationship, celebrated every year with a festival called *Raksha Bandhan*. On this day, a girl ties a bracelet called a *rakhi* on her brother's wrist. In return, he promises to protect and help her if she is ever in need. Boys who do not have sisters are "adopted" by female cousins who tie on rakhis or send them by mail to wherever they are.

Indian Mothers and Fathers

Indian women are well known for their spirit of sacrifice and devotion. Mothers are especially respected in Indian society. Cows are sacred because they are a symbol of motherhood. *Mata* means "mother." Important rivers such as the Ganges are called mata, too.

Indian parents give their whole lives to raising their children. In turn, they expect their children to take care of them in their old age. Since there are no senior citizen homes in India, grandparents usually live in the same house with their sons.

Grandparents are an important part of an Indian family. In a busy household, Grandma always has the time to listen to a child, to tell a story, or to protect the child from an angry parent. In turn, children gladly run errands for their grandparents.

Often, brothers live in a common home with their wives, children, and parents. This is called a joint family. Children who grow up in joint families have lots of fun. They have plenty of cousins to play with and are never lonely. There are many loving adults to care for their needs. Children are the center of every household. Parents seldom go out without them.

Special Ceremonies

Ceremonies mark many events in an Indian's life. The birth of a child is a very happy occasion. Streams of visitors come to see the baby and congratulate the family. Often many people are invited to the *Naam-*

Families, Homes, and Foods

karan, the naming ceremony for a baby. (However, birthdays are usually not celebrated in India, except by more modern families in cities.)

There are also religious ceremonies for Indian children. Hindu boys have their heads shaved at the *Mundan* ceremony, because Hindus believe it is unhealthy and unlucky to keep the hair you are born with. On the other hand, Sikh children are not supposed to cut their hair. When Sikh boys are five, they are given their first *puggree* (turban), such as older boys and men wear, after a ceremony called *Dastar Bandi*. And in *Amrit Chakana* Sikh teenagers go to their temple to take the vows of Sikhism.

Zoroastrian children have a *Navjot* ceremony, where they are given special clothes and recite prayers with their priests. Muslim children first learn about the *Koran*, their holy book, in the *Bismillah* ceremony. Later, before they are thirteen years old, they learn how to fast for the month of Ramadan in a special ceremony called the *Roza Rakha*.

Indian Weddings

Nowhere are family and ceremony tied together more firmly than at a marriage. Even though more modern Indians pick their own marriage partners,

A traditional Hindu wedding: the groom arrives at the head of the baraat *riding a decorated horse* (left). *During the wedding ceremony, the couple puts several offerings into the sacred fire and takes seven steps around it, while a priest recites the ceremony in Sanskrit* (right).

this is not so for more traditional Indians. Many boys and girls do not date in India; rather, their marriages are arranged by their parents and relatives. Since Indians believe that marriages should last a lifetime, families look carefully at a possible bride or groom's relatives and their reputation. They believe that people act as they see others act while they are growing up. These children believe that their families will make good choices when a partner is picked for them.

The bride and groom under a canopy of flowers. Weddings like these usually are held outdoors at night.

Indian weddings are quite different from what Americans are used to. The wedding takes place at the bride's home. The groom, dressed as a warrior, ride on a beautifully decorated horse. Behind him sits a young boy, usually a nephew, dressed like him. Following the horse is a long line of the groom's relatives. This procession is called a *baraat*. When the baraat arrives outside the bride's home, the bride's relatives welcome them. The bride's grandfather greets the groom's grandfather with a hug; then fathers, brothers, and uncles embrace and put wreaths, or garlands, on each other. Finally, the bride and the groom garland each other. Then the cere-

There are mud huts in poorer sections of India...

mony can begin. As you can see, an Indian marriage is not just the wedding of two people; it is the union of two families!

Many Kinds of Homes

Once a couple is married, how they will live depends on whether they are well to do, middle class, or poor, and whether they live in a village or city. Well-

and very modern buildings in big cities like New Delhi.

to-do families live in large homes. They have cars, televisions, and servants. Middle-class families live in smaller houses or in apartments called flats.

Poor folk live in huts made of bricks and mud with thatched roofs. These villagers line the walls of their huts with mud and cow dung, then whitewash (paint) them with lime. They might decorate the outside of their home with pictures of birds and animals. Inside, the walls are usually bare, except for a picture of Krishna or Rama and a hook on which to hang clothes. Often, the only furniture in the home is a *charpie*, a wooden bed with knotted string in place of a mattress. People usually sit, work, and eat on the floor or on straw mats.

Most homes have a walled courtyard which is like a family room. Children play here, and old folks sit on their charpies and pass the time. (The family cow may also live here or may be tied up outside the hut.)

Huts in rainy, swampy areas are built on tall poles. In hilly, snowy areas, homes are made of wood and have sloping roofs. But mostly, Indian houses for the more well off are made of bricks and concrete. They do not have basements or underground cellars. They usually have a flat roof called a terrace, with a waist-high ledge around it.

In the summer Indians like to sleep on the terrace on charpies. Every morning, or if it rains at night, bedding is rolled up and the charpies are stacked together in a storeroom. Large houses often have a small, separate apartment for the family servant, called the servant's quarter.

Housework and Cooking

A middle-class Indian homemaker has many helpers. Even if she does not have a full-time helper

Indians love to sleep outdoors on charpies, usually placed on the flat rooftop terraces of homes.

who cooks and cleans, she may have several part-time helpers: one to do the dishes, another to clean the house, and so on. Most Indian homes do not have the gadgets that we are used to—vacuum cleaners, dishwashers, or washing machines.

The washing of clothes is usually done by laundry men called *dhobis*. The dhobi comes to the house once or twice a week to take dirty clothes, and brings them back the following week, washed, ironed, and neatly folded. Often a dhobi sets up shop on a street corner with a table and a heavy iron filled with hot coals. A woman who wants her sari ironed in a hurry will send it to him to be pressed within minutes.

Indian women do not have to leave their homes to buy fruits and vegetables, because at least one vegetable seller will be by, calling out his or her wares. The seller walks or cycles down the street with a basket of fresh fruits and vegetables. He or she sets down the basket on the doorstep and talks about the wonderful things in the basket. After a little bargaining, the woman will purchase what she needs for the day's meals.

Favorite Indian Foods

Preparing an Indian meal takes time and trouble because most things have to be done by hand. Onions have to be ground to a paste on a grinding stone, for most Indian dishes are based on an onion-spice mixture that has to be browned in oil. Meat or vegetables are added to this roasted mixture and cooked with water until tender. This is called a meat or vegetable *curry*.

A curry is any dish that has a gravy and that is flavored with a mixture of typical Indian spices. The most commonly used spice in Indian cooking is turmeric, which turns food yellow. Other favorite spices are ground cumin and coriander seeds. Just a bit of expensive spices such as cardamoms, cloves, and cinnamon is used in meat curries.

Meat is also expensive, and few families can afford to eat it every day. Since Hindus do not eat beef and Muslims do not eat pork, meat curries are made from goat meat or chicken. Chicken that has been grilled in an earthenware oven called a *tandoor* is a great favorite in northern India.

Most Indians are vegetarians. Two out of three eat rice daily. With this they usually take a bowl of lentil soup called *dal*. There are many different kinds of lentils—red, green, yellow, or black. South Indians eat a hot, spicy dal called *sambhar*. With it they enjoy paper-thin rice-flour pancakes.

Most north Indians eat some form of *roti* at least once a day. Roti is a round, flat pancake-like bread. There are different ways of making roti. Sometimes corn flour is added to the dough. Sometimes balls of dough are dropped into boiling oil, where they puff up into round, hollow balls. These puffed-up rotis are eaten on festive days with *halwa*, a favorite sweet.

The rotis eaten on ordinary days are most often baked on a black iron griddle. These are called *chappattis*. Chappattis are sometimes stuffed with grated vegetables and fried in a little oil. This dish is *paranthas*. Some people like to eat paranthas with yoghurt

Many Indian villagers depend on wells for water for cooking and cleaning.

for brunch. But poor people are used to eating plain dal and rotis every day.

Those who can afford it like to eat dishes made from milk. *Panir* is a homemade cheese which is started by adding lemon juice to boiling milk. The milk curdles, or turns into small lumps. The curds are strained through a fine cloth and placed under a heavy weight until they begin to stick together. Then the

Families, Homes, and Foods

panir can be cut up, deep fried, and curried with peas and potatoes.

Yoghurt is another favorite milk dish. Housewives like to make a pot of yoghurt every day. Sometimes chopped or grated vegetables are added to yoghurt to make *raita*. Yoghurt is also used in a favorite Punjabi drink called *lassi*. A cup of water and a cup of yoghurt, beaten until bubbly, makes this cooling drink for a hot day.

Sherbet is a popular summertime drink. Differently flavored, colorful syrups are sold in bottles. Cold water is added to a few tablespoons of the syrup to make the drink. But on both hot days and cold days Indians love to drink a cup or glass of steaming hot tea. When guests come to the home, they are at least offered a cup of tea or a glass of sherbet. Even though alcohol is not forbidden to Hindus, as it is to Muslims, it is almost never served. Wine is not drunk with meals; instead, most people have a glass of cold water with their dinner.

Inside Indian Kitchens

Indian plates, called *thalis*, are usually made of steel. In a thali one can place many little steel bowls, each containing a small serving of the foods prepared.

In an Indian kitchen most utensils, even glasses, are made of steel or brass.

Instead of using paper plates, Indians use banana leaves which have been cut into squares. These can be thrown away when you are done eating. Cheap, disposable clay cups are made by the hundreds by potters. These are used to carry home prepared food from shops. They can be smashed and thrown away when they are no longer needed.

But few things are thrown out in an Indian home. Even the well-to-do have no throw-aways like paper towels, plastic wrap, or aluminum foil. Tin, glass, and paper are all expensive and hard to get in India, and people are used to saving them. This is why canned foods are rarely found in Indian kitchens.

Modern Indian kitchens have gas or electric stoves. Others have small earthenware stoves called *chulhas.* Poor people just light a fire between two bricks. Because much cooking is done on the floor, the floor has to be kept clean. Every night, the kitchen is washed and the water pushed through a drain in the floor with a broom. A typical Indian kitchen is almost a sacred place, like a temple. No one may enter it with his or her shoes on!

Indian table manners are quite different from ours, because often Indians do not eat at a table as we do. Except for modern townspeople, most Indians eat

Families, Homes, and Foods

their meals on the floor. They do not use forks and knives either, but prefer to eat with their hands. Indian children learn to wrap a piece of roti around the meat or vegetable, and then dip it in dal and eat it.

Indians like eating hot, freshly prepared food. The family sits crosslegged on the floor around the mother while she makes rotis on the chulha stove. Turn by turn, each person gets a roti just as soon as it is ready.

Although you probably don't own a chulha, you can make some Indian foods yourself. Here is a recipe for chappattis, the flat roti that is eaten every day by millions of Indians.

Chappattis

2 cups whole wheat flour
1/2 teaspoon salt
2 tablespoons melted butter or margarine
3/8 cup water
A heavy skillet

1. Mix the flour and salt in a bowl. Add the butter or margarine and 3/4 of the water. Mix this dough together. If it is still too dry to hold

together in a ball, add a little more water to the mixture. (You do not necessarily need to use all the water.)

2. Knead the dough, pushing it down and folding it over. Do this for about five minutes. Then cover the kneaded dough with a damp towel and let it sit for one hour.

3. Uncover the dough and knead it for another minute or two. Then break the dough into round balls, each about the size of a golf ball.

4. Take each small ball and turn it into a flat circle about 1/4 inch thick. You can pat it flat with your hands (be sure to flour your hands first) or use a rolling pin, putting the dough on a floured surface. When each chappatti is flat, put a dusting of flour on it.

5. Heat the skillet. Cook each chappatti for two minutes on each side. When all the chappattis have been cooked this way, brush the skillet with some butter or margarine and lightly brown each piece.

Chappattis should be eaten hot off the griddle!

Chappattis are baked on stoves. Here, chappattis are being prepared for a large gathering of people.

Raita is another easy dish to make.

Cucumber Raita

1 medium-sized cucumber
2 cups yoghurt
1/2 teaspoon salt
A grater

1. Grate the cucumber coarsely. Squeeze the grated cucumber until it is fairly dry.

2. Add the salt to the yoghurt. Then stir in the cucumber.

7. A Respect for Learning

When Bengali children are old enough to write, they go through a little ceremony during the spring festival honoring Saraswati, the goddess of learning. There, before her image, the children trace their first letter. This custom is common in other parts of India, too, among families who value knowledge and learning.

In ancient India, only sons of Brahmins (priests) and Kshatriyas (warriors) received an education. At the age of seven or eight these boys went to live in their guru's (teacher's) homes. They lived there for many years until the gurus had taught them all they needed to know—hunting skills, the art of warfare, reading, writing, and knowledge from the holy books. All other boys stayed home and learned their fathers' trades.

Education for All

Much later, in the 1800s, the British began bringing Western education to Indians. The British government and Christian missionary groups started many schools and colleges which taught Western knowledge and science in the English language. Education spread to the middle classes.

Still, an education was not available to everyone. Many villages had no schools at all. Children of farmers, weavers, and untouchables had no choice but to follow their parents' occupations. The poor remained poor.

In order to close the gap between the rich and the poor, India's government today is trying hard to provide basic education for everyone. In 1950, only 16 percent of the population could read and write. Today 36.7 percent of Indians are literate. When India became independent, only 33 percent of children between the ages of six and eleven went to school. Today, nearly 87 percent attend primary school.

University education is planned so that even the poorest can attend college. A certain portion of places are reserved in every college for more disadvantaged students—women and students from tribal areas and lower castes. This way, the son of a potter can become an engineer. Many women become doctors. Of all college students in India, 27 percent are women.

School—A New Tradition

Still, many children, especially girls, never go to school at all. Others drop out very quickly. Most of these children live in backward areas or belong to tribes or the lowest castes. Girls are often kept at home to look after younger brothers and sisters.

To encourage these youngsters to attend school, many state governments provide them with scholarships, free textbooks, and free midday meals. Preschools and day-care centers are being opened in some states. This way, a young girl can leave her baby brother in the center and attend school herself. Also, children who attend preschool do not drop out of school as often or as quickly because they are better prepared for formal schooling.

Formal schooling—reading and math—often do not have much meaning for a child who lives in a crowded hut and doesn't get enough to eat. The government has started non-formal education centers for such children. Here they learn how to stay clean, strong, and healthy every day.

Still another way of educating villagers is through television and radio. Scientists hope to broadcast nationwide instructional television through a satellite. Right now, educational programs are being beamed to 1,200 villages via stations on the ground. Radio is used to train teachers in some states. The government is trying everything possible to bring education to all Indian children, no matter how poor or how remote their village.

(Above) *In villages, children study under the trees.* (Below) *Television helps bring education to even far-away villages and towns.*

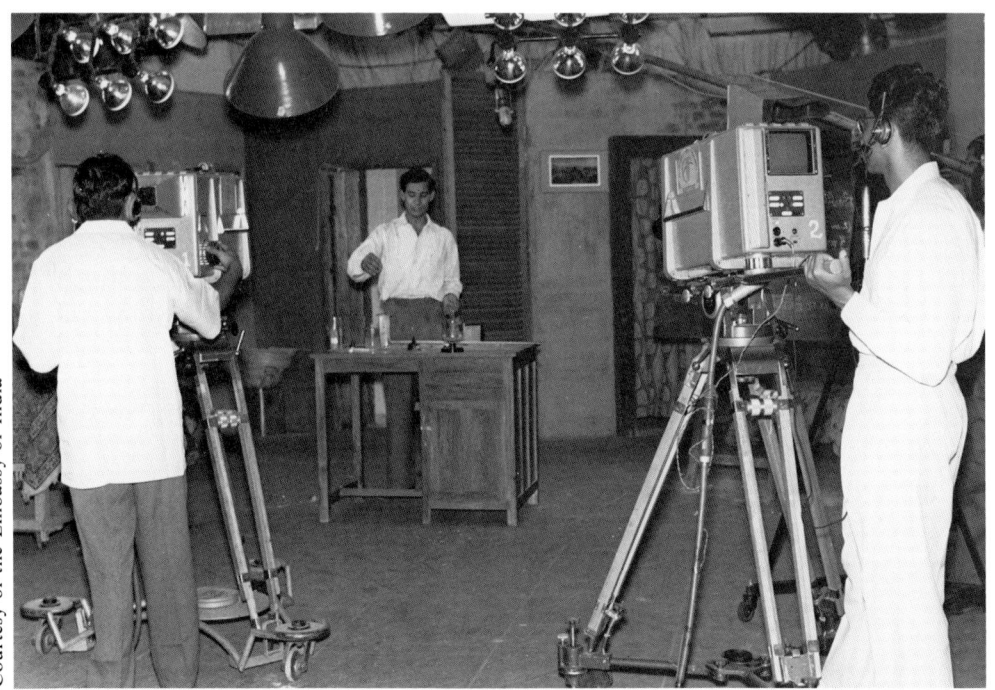

Village and city schools are usually run by the state or city government. Some families send their children to private schools. Although many private schools are run by Christian missionaries, most of the children who go there are not Christians. While government-run schools are usually free or very inexpensive, private schools can be quite costly.

Village Classrooms

City schools are quite different from village schools. City schools, especially private ones, usually have large brick buildings with athletic fields and many classrooms. A village school may have only a single room for all grades, or perhaps no room at all. Then classes have to be held outdoors, under the trees. In such schools, you can hear the children study because they chant their lessons out loud. The entire class recites multiplication tables or the alphabet, led by the teacher or by one of the students.

In village schools, children sit on rows of rough floor mats; in private schools, they sit on chairs, and every student has a desk to himself or herself. Most desk tops have a square hollow in the corner for a bottle of ink. Children usually write with fountain pens or pens that have to be dipped in ink. Village children write on slates (small chalkboards) with

A Respect for Learning

chalk. Others write with ink on white wooden boards. Every night, the board has to be whitened with lime so that it can be used again the next day.

Paper, Pen, and Ink

Paper and books are expensive in India and are used carefully. Even in wealthier private schools, children do not get mimeographed worksheets as do American children. This is because photocopying and mimeographing are also very expensive. Children do their homework and classwork in notebooks called copies or exercise books. Children usually have separate copies for each subject. To keep them neat, copies and textbooks are covered with brown paper in the beginning of the school year.

Textbooks are also expensive; children usually sell them to a secondhand bookshop at the end of the year. At these shops book binders re-stitch loose pages and fit old books with new covers. School children cannot make use of free public libraries either, as we do. Overall there are almost 26,000 libraries in the United States, but there are only 10,000 in India for almost three times as many people.

Books are sacred to Indians. If a child drops a book or accidentally steps on one, he or she will quickly pick it up. Then he may touch it to his forehead or she may kiss it as a mark of respect.

Some girls have to care for younger brothers and sisters, making it very hard for them to attend school.

Respect for Teachers

Teachers, too, are treated with respect in Indian schools. Reverence for teachers is an ancient Indian tradition. Because a guru was older, and because he alone was the source of all knowledge, he was obeyed and honored by his students. Indeed, he was not just respected, but worshipped. This was called *guru-bhakti*. You can see this respect in a story from the *Mahabharata*.

Families, Homes, and Foods

Dronacharya was guru to the Pandava princes. He was famous for his skill in teaching the arts of warfare. Eklavya, a tribal prince, begged Drona to teach him to be an expert archer like Arjuna, the third Pandava prince. But Drona turned Eklavya away; Drona had promised Arjuna that no one would ever be better than him in archery. Some time later, Drona and his pupils heard of an expert archer so skilled he could perform miracles with his bow and arrow. They hurried to see him at work. They found Eklavya, practicing archery in the woods. Near him was a clay image of Drona. In his heart, Eklavya thought of Drona as his guru and bowed before his statue every day. It was this spirit of devotion and respect for his teacher that had helped him become an expert.

The famous *sitar* player, Ravi Shankar, also had a guru—Ustad Allauddin Khan, India's finest musician. In order to be Khan's student, Ravi Shankar left Paris, where he had lived for many years, for his guru's tiny village in India. For several years he lived there, devoted to his sitar and his guru.

Though they may not be as devoted as Eklavya or Ravi Shankar, modern Indian students are also polite and respectful to their teachers. Teachers are never called by their first names; "ji" is often added to their names. When a teacher walks into the room, the entire class stands up to greet him or her. They may say "Namaste" or "Jai Hind" (victory to India). Convent children say "Good Morning" to their teachers.

Missionary schools for girls are called convents and are run by nuns. Primary schools are often coeducational, but later, boys and girls usually go to separate schools. Convent schools are known for their high standards of education and strict rules. Children there are always quiet, well behaved, and neatly dressed.

Schools in the City

Most city schools have uniforms. Girls wear Indian clothes. Boys wear pants or shorts with shirts. Convent girls usually wear Western clothes—skirts and blouses, with blazers during the winter. Some schools are very strict about uniforms. Buttons, belts, socks, and ribbons have to be of the correct school color. Shoes have to be clean and polished. A child may be sent home for not being in uniform, or punished for wearing dirty shoes.

Children are also punished for not doing their homework, for being late to school, or for talking in class. As a punishment, the child may have to stand facing the wall in the corner of the room. Another form of punishment is "lines." A child may have to write "I will not talk in class" one hundred times.

Silence during class is considered very important. If the teacher leaves the room for a few minutes, he or she leaves a monitor in charge. The monitor or captain is a child who is selected by the teacher or by the other children to be the leader of the class or "house."

City schools and classes are usually divided into four or six houses or groups. The houses are named after historical figures and heroes (Asoka House, Shiva ji House, etc.). Each house has its own flag, color, and captain. Competitions among houses are organized every year for activities such as music, speech, drama, and sports. On Sports Day or Annual Day, children of all ages march with their house. They wear a band of their house color and follow the house captain who carries the house flag. The entire school gets together to enjoy the marching and sports events.

In most schools, students and teachers get together every morning after the bell rings for assembly. Here prayers are said, announcements are made, and uniforms are inspected. Some schools have a short class period after assembly where values and current events can be discussed. The central government is working on courses in moral education; all school children can be taught values like honesty, fairness,

Indian students often wear uniforms to school.

and pride in their nation. In this way the government hopes to start a common Indian spirit in children from different backgrounds who speak different languages.

Languages Children Study

School children in India today are taught three languages. According to Prime Minister Nehru's three-language plan, the regional language must be taught at the primary school level. Hindi and English are taught later. In Hindi-speaking states, Sanskrit is offered as a third language.

But how and when the three languages are taught differs not only from state to state, but also from

The Indian government is trying hard to provide education for everyone, even for these children from poor sections of a city (who in earlier times would not have had a chance to go to school).

school to school. Village children may learn only a little Hindi and English. Missionary schools and other private schools teach in English from the first grade. Children educated in such schools speak English very well and can get good jobs. This is why good private schools are very hard to get into. Many students apply for every seat available. Some families go to great trouble to get their child admitted to the school of their choice.

However, one does not have to attend a fancy private school to do well. Nobel Prize winner Dr. Har Gobind Khorana got the first four years of his schooling in a village school under the trees! Government schools also have good standards of education, and many of their students go on to become lawyers, teachers, and other professionals.

High Schools and Colleges

Most secondary (high) schools are controlled by a national board of education. This board inspects schools, sets standards for hiring teachers, and decides what students will study. It also makes up and grades the final, qualifying exams that all students must pass before graduating from high school.

Schools run by this board have these final exams at two levels—the tenth grade and the twelfth grade. This is called the 10 + 2 system. Students who do not wish to go to college leave after they pass the tenth-grade exam. Those who wish to qualify for college stay in school until the twelfth grade exam.

There are 111 universities and 3,000 colleges in India today, six times the number in the country at independence. Three million students train to be doctors, engineers, scientists, teachers, and administrators. But this is only 4 percent of Indians between the ages of seventeen and twenty-five. To get into a good college, especially medical school, a student has to get good grades in the qualifying examinations.

Tests, Tests, Tests

Students who pass the exams are placed in first, second, or third divisions, depending on what grades they got. The quality of a school is often judged by the number of first and second division students it graduates every year.

Final exams are very important throughout school life. A student who fails the final exam cannot be promoted to the next grade. Most examination questions have to be answered in writing. Multiple-choice or true-false types of questions are not common. School children have to be able to write well to do well in examinations.

Final exams are usually given in April or May before the two-month summer vacation. The weeks before exams are spent in serious study—called "mugging" or "cramming." Some students get extra help from parents or private tutors. Others get together with friends to review the year's work. There is less playing and laughter. Households become quiet.

Learning is a serious business in India. To some it is worthy of worship. Indians value books because they treasure knowledge. They revere (honor) teachers because they respect learning. This is the heart of the Indian attitude towards education: reverence and respect.

8. "Kabbaddi, Kabbaddi, Kabbaddi...."

When Indian children get home from school, they change out of their uniforms and do their homework. Then they can run out to the nearest *maidan* (playground) and join their friends in a game of cricket.

Cricket is thought of as the national game of India, as popular there as baseball and football are here. Cricket is like both sports in some ways. A cricket team has eleven players, like a football team. Cricket is played with a bat and ball and has innings, like baseball.

But in cricket the bat is long and flat instead of rounded. The batter is the "batsman" and the pitcher is the "bowler." The "infield" is not a diamond but a rectangle. There is no home plate—instead, there are two wickets, constructed of three waist-high poles with small sticks called bails lying on top of them. The bowler pitches (bowls), trying to knock the bails off the wicket to get the batsman out. The batsman swings at the pitch, trying to keep it away from the wicket and send it out beyond the infield. When the ball is hit, the batsman and another of his or her teammates (who's been standing at the opposite wicket) run back and forth between the wickets to

In cricket, the batsman (standing) *tries to keep the ball from knocking the bails off the wicket behind him or her.*

score runs. They can run until the other team throws back the ball and knocks a bail off a wicket. A team's inning is over when ten batsmen are out. Then the other team has its turn at bat.

A cricket game is called a match. Matches vary in length. A cricket match can last for five days or more! In such a match, hundreds of runs are scored before it is over. The team that scores the most runs wins.

Field hockey is popular in India. Indian teams have won gold medals for field hockey in many Olympic competitions.

Team Sports in India

Indian adults play cricket, too. Indian teams often visit countries like Australia, Great Britain, and the West Indies to play matches. Also, the teams play other teams from different parts of India to win prizes and trophies. The most famous of these is the Ranji Trophy.

Whether the match is at home or abroad, Indians everywhere are interested in the results. Sometimes matches are on radio or television. Then people gather in the bazaars to listen to them. Bicyclists hold transistor radios to their ears as they pedal along. When people meet each other, they ask, "What's the score?" In 1983 the Indian team beat the West Indians to win the World Cup for cricket. The Indian fans went crazy. They celebrated by setting off firecrackers!

But the game for which India is really well known is field hockey. India has won the gold medal for field hockey in at least eight Olympic competitions. In the United States, field hockey teams try to copy the Indian playing styles.

Another popular team sport in India is soccer, known as football there. (When Indians visit the United States, they are surprised to see how different American football is from their "football"!) Soccer teams all over India play each other for the Santosh Trophy. Teams from other countries are invited to play in the Nehru Gold Cup Tournament.

Jawahar Lal Nehru, India's first prime minister, enjoyed cricket, swimming, trekking (hiking), and riding. He wanted Indians to take an active part in international sports. Therefore, the first Asian Games (or Asiad) were held in India in 1951 while he was prime minister. In 1982, the ninth Asian Games were played in New Delhi. Six thousand sports men and women from thirty-three different countries took part in sixteen days of competition and fun.

The Indian government built many huge sports arenas in New Delhi for the Games. The new Cultural Complex has a large auditorium with a very good sound system and stage. Here Indians can now enjoy operas and symphonies. An Olympic-sized pool was constructed for the Asiad, as was a huge indoor stadium. A 75,000-seat outdoor stadium was named after Nehru and was opened on his birthday, November 14. (Because Nehru loved children, his birthday is also observed as Children's Day.)

Children's Sports and Games

Indian schoolchildren play cricket, field hockey, and soccer. They also play basketball, volleyball, and net ball. School teams play against each other in tournaments. Junior leagues from different zones and regions of the country compete for national championships. Students stay after school to train for the teams. They also have time during the school day for physical training (P.T.). P.T. includes exercises, gymnastics, relay races, athletics, games, and sports.

Indian women also take an active part in sports. School girls swim and play basketball, volleyball, soccer, hockey, and cricket. They play just about anything that boys play, even at an international level.

At lunch breaks and after school, children get together to play games. *Kho* is a game popular with Indian children. Players are divided into two equal teams. Team A sits in a line with every other player facing in opposite directions. Team B children run about. One of the runners pushes one of the sitters and yells, "Kho." The sitter then jumps up and chases the Team B runners. Anyone he or she touches is out of the game. The Team A player can also push his or her squatting teammates with a "Kho!" and get them to chase after the Team B players until they have all been caught.

In *Kabbaddi* two equal-sized teams face each other across a line. A player from Team A has to run across the line, tag a Team B player, and make it back to his or her side without being caught by the "enemy." All this has to be done on a single breath! To prove they have not taken another breath, the players chant "Kabbaddi-Kabbaddi-Kabbaddi..." until they get back to his or her team. If they can even touch the dividing line after being tagged by the enemy, and are still chanting, "Kabbaddi," all the Team B players who touched them are out of the game. Therefore, Team B has to be careful not to tag a player until that person is cornered and cannot get to the line in the

Soccer, like cricket, has many enthusiastic Indian fans.

same breath. To be good at Kabbaddi, you have to be clever, quick, and good at holding your breath!

Kabbaddi competitions are popular in villages and towns in most parts of India. Recently, Kabbaddi teams from other Asian countries visited India. Though it is mainly an Indian sport, it is catching on elsewhere.

Made in India

India has imported many games and sports from other nations. Cricket is an English game, and basketball came from America. But many sports and games that we know today began in India.

Polo is a sport that began in India and spread to other countries. In 1862 British army officers watched some tribal horsemen with long sticks pushing a ball made of willow leaves, called a *pulu*. Soon the British made up their own game of polo which became very popular in England. An American millionaire who watched the game in England took it to America.

Badminton also came to America from India. An English earl introduced this Indian game, called *poona*, to his English friends at Badminton, his estate in England. Badminton became very popular in England and America. It is a racquet game similar to tennis, but, instead of a ball, a feathered shuttlecock is used. Since no special court is needed, families often put up a net in the yard and play badminton in the evenings with friends and neighbors.

Indians have long believed that physical fitness is important. In ancient times, Indian kings often arranged tournaments in archery or athletics to choose a husband for their daughters. In order to win battles and win wives, men had to be strong and skilled in the fighting arts. Chariot racing, swimming, wrestling, and archery were popular sports. It is said that Lord Krishna loved to swim, and Buddha was an excellent archer.

Yoga has its beginning in Vedic (Aryan) teaching. Teachers of yoga believe that the mind and the body are strongly linked together. In order to be truly healthy, people have to be totally aware of their bodies and should also be able to control them with their minds. *Raja yoga* is a kind of yoga which shows how to develop a strong will and controlled mind through meditation. *Hatha yoga* is a form of Raja yoga and teaches various postures and breathing exercises which are good for various parts of the body. Yoga schools and exercise programs are popular not only in India today, but all over the world.

Some popular games also came from India. Chess began here many centuries ago and then spread to the rest of the world. Mughal Emperor Akbar loved the game very much. In his capital at Fatehpur Sikri, he had a special checkered floor built. Here he played a form of human chess, with real human beings acting as chess pieces. In modern India, players compete for the National Chess Championship and play in the All-India Chess Tournament.

"Snakes and Ladders" is a children's game very similar to "Chutes and Ladders," the American game. American children also like to play Parcheesi, which began in ancient India. It is said that even Lord Shiva played Parcheesi, which used to be known as *chaupar*. Chaupar was also a favorite with kings.

From Health Clubs to Empty Lots

Kings and other wealthy Indians had the time and money to become good at various sports. Wealthy Indians belong to golf clubs, polo clubs, yacht clubs, and health clubs. Upper-middle-class families belong to clubs where their children can swim, play tennis, or learn to ride.

Village children and the poor in cities do not have such places. Compared to our country, India has very few playgrounds, swimming pools, tennis courts, or gymnasiums. In our country, the county or the state offers affordable classes and after-school programs. Such classes are not available to most Indian children.

Still, the children have each other. Older children look after their younger brothers and sisters and make sure no one bullies them. They gather in groups to play on dusty maidans and manage to have a very good time. Because they have so little, poor children learn early to make do with what they can find. For a swing, they'll attach a plank to a rope and hang it from a tree. Many of their games require very little equipment. Sometimes neighborhood children pool their money to buy a cricket bat, ball, and wickets, which they all share. But even if they cannot afford bats and balls, children make up games using sticks and stones and still have fun.

Courtesy of the Embassy of India

India still does not have enough sports facilities for its large population. Private clubs, like the one at which tennis star Vijay Amritraj is shown, are few in number; most children have to use their imaginations in order to find things to do.

"Kabbaddi, Kabbaddi, Kabbaddi. . . ."

Gulli-danda is a popular game played with sticks. The *gulli* is a small stick pointed at both ends, and the *danda* is a longer stick. The batter strikes the gulli with the danda. When it flies up in the air, he or she strikes it again. The player who sends the gulli farthest wins.

Gitta is a game similar to jacks which is played with stones or dried beans. Five stones are thrown on the ground. One is tossed in the air. The idea is to pick up a stone and catch the falling stone before it hits the ground. In the next round, two stones have to be picked up without touching any of the other stones. It is a game that requires practice and skill.

Another game of skill is marbles. Children take turns shooting marbles with a flick of the finger into a hole in the ground. The winner gets to keep the marbles shot into the hole.

Stores also usually carry a good supply of paper kites and plenty of kite string. Indian kites are usually diamond shaped and come in bright colors. The kite string is often coated with powdered glass. This is because children try to cut each other's kites down. Children go up to the rooftops or run along a maidan letting the kite go higher and higher until someone yells, "Wo Kata!" (cut) and the kite comes drifting down to the ground.

Both rich and poor children enjoy kites, marbles, gulli-danda, kho, and kabbaddi. But neither have the kinds of chances that American children have. The Indian government is trying hard to improve the lives of Indian children—a difficult task and a very important one. India has close to 300 million children.

Imagine that! India has more children than America has people. Forty-two percent of the Indian population is under the age of fifteen. Only sixty million Americans, 25 percent of our population, are in the same age group.

In the future, more money will be spent on providing sports and recreational facilities for everyone. The Indian government realizes that the children of India need chances to develop their minds and bodies and learn new skills. Then they will show the world what they can do.

9. The Jet Generation

Anita lives in Maryland, where she was born. Her parents were born and brought up in India; twenty years ago they moved to the United States. Anita has an uncle in London, aunts in Maryland and New York, and grandparents in India. Her parents have cousins in Hong Kong, Canada, and Saudi Arabia. Many of Anita's Indian friends also have relatives all over the world.

Today, Indians are a people on the move. The number of places in which they've settled is amazing.

For centuries, Indians remained in their own country, except for those who settled in neighboring nations such as Malaysia and Sri Lanka. Some never saw anything but their own small village and the surrounding land. Many Hindus believed they would lose their caste if they crossed the ocean. Few ever did leave. Instead, people from other lands came to India, to trade, to raid, to rule, and to live. For thousands of years, India took in people of different races and religions, mixed them up in a melting pot, and made them its own.

In the last two centuries, the tables have turned. Indians are leaving their overcrowded homeland in search of better opportunities and better lives. Today they have immigrated to more than fifty countries around the world, including the United States.

But the Indians in the United States number less than half a million, and most of them have not been here very long. Although immigration from India to the United States began in 1820, only about 7,000 Indians had arrived by 1920. Most of these were Punjabi Sikh farmers who came hoping to earn extra money for their families back home. Canadian steamship companies tried to bring over Indian laborers to work on railroads and farms in western Canada and the United States.

By that time, thousands of unskilled Chinese laborers had arrived in California, willing to work for low wages. Local American workers were afraid that Asians would drive down their wages and take their jobs. They formed the Asiatic Exclusion League, which demanded that Asian immigration be stopped. In 1924, the American government passed the Johnson-Reid Act, setting the number of immigrants allowed from each country. According to this law, two immigrants would be admitted every year for every hundred of the same nationality already living in the States. Two percent of the tiny number of Indians in the United States meant few Indian immigrants. In the next twenty years only 423 Indians arrived here.

Meanwhile, Asians here were not treated very well. Restaurants and hotels refused to serve them. They were not allowed to own property or to become citizens. As a result, many Indians left the United States. In the first half of this century, 9,000 Indians arrived here, but 6,600 returned to India.

An Indian named Dalip Singh Saund did much to obtain political rights for Asians in America. In 1946, he succeeded in having Congress pass a bill allowing Asians to become American citizens. In 1956, he became the first Asian ever to be elected to the Congress of the United States. He served three terms. Saund loved America, where he had lived since 1920, but he never forgot India. He was called the "Congressman from India." He always spoke up in favor of independence for India from British rule.

Many other educated Indians also disliked British rule. Some of them came to California as students. They wanted Indians in the United States to return to India and lead a rebellion against the British. Helped by some of the rich Punjabi farmers, these students formed a group called the *Ghadar* (mutiny) Party. The leaders, Har Dayal and Taraknath Das, published a newspaper called *Ghadar*, written in many Indian languages. The American government did not like their activities; in 1918, several Ghadar members were put in jail.

Over the years, American feelings towards Indian and Asian immigration changed a great deal. The nations of the world depended more and more on each other for trade. It no longer made sense to keep out people from one part of the world. President John F. Kennedy spoke out against the immigration laws. In 1965, the Johnson-Reid Act was abolished.

Still, there were only 387,223 Indians in the United States in 1980. In 1970, when the number of people in America was counted, Indians were not even described as a separate group of people. Now they are called "Asian Indians" so as not to confuse them with American Indians. Because of a mistake a long time ago, the term *Indian* is a very confusing one in the world today.

When Christopher Columbus set out to discover a sea route to India, he found America. Thinking he had arrived in India, he named the islands the Indies and their people, the Indians. The name stuck. Today those islands are called the West Indies and their people are West Indians. Therefore, Indians from India are often called East Indians. But East Indians are really Bengalis and Orrissis—the people of eastern India!

However, Asian Indians in America represent every region, religion, and language of India. Punjabi Sikhs, Bengali Muslims, Gujarati Jains, and Kerala

Christians are sprinkled all over the country. Asian Indians who lived in the West Indies, Africa, and England have also immigrated to America. For the most part, Indians here live in and around big cities. Over sixty thousand live in New York state. Large numbers of Indians live in the states of Illinois, New Jersey, Texas, Pennsylvania, Michigan, and Maryland. About sixty thousand live in California.

California has some of the oldest Indian communities in the United States. About two thousand families, mainly Punjabi Sikhs, own farms in and around Yuba City and Stockton. Some families have lived here for generations. Didar Singh Bains, who arrived in 1958 to join his father and grandfather, started out as an ordinary farm laborer. Today, he owns several thousand acres of farmland, and is said to be California's largest peach grower.

But the California farmers are not typical of the Indians in the United States. A great many of the Asian Indians here are doctors, scientists, or engineers because our immigration laws let in members of certain professions more often than others. This is why 52 percent of the Asian Indian adults here have four or more years of college education. (Only 16.23 percent of American adults have as much schooling.) The average income in 1980 of an Indian family was $29,591 to the national average of $23,092.

Is it strange that people from a "poor" country like India should be among the richest in the richest nation in the world? Not when you realize that Asian Indians in the United States come from educated, middle-class city families in India. Few, if any, grew up in a mud hut. They did not leave India because they were starving or being jailed. They came to the United States looking for more education and better chances in life.

Although India has the third largest number of trained people in the world, it cannot yet provide satisfying jobs for all of them, especially those who receive their training abroad. Some do go back and apply their American training to Indian needs. Others prefer to remain here because in America their talent has taken root and flowered.

Indians who have come to the United States have a reputation for excellence in every field. Punjabi scientist Dr. Har Gobind Khorana shared the 1968 Nobel Prize in Medicine for helping figure out how our genes work. Two years later, he made the world's first artificial gene. In 1983, Dr. Subrahmanyan Chandrasekhar of Tamil Nadu shared the Nobel Prize for Physics. Zubin Mehta, who is an Indian Parsee, leads the New York Philharmonic, one of America's finest orchestras. Computer parts are manufactured by California millionaire S. L. Tandon,

Dr. Subrahmanyan Chandrasekhar won a Nobel Prize in Physics in 1983.

who has sixty millionaires working for him. Author Ved Mehta is editor of the *New Yorker* magazine and has written many books about his childhood in India. Science writer Gobind Behari Lal won the Pulitzer Prize years ago. Olympic gold medalist Alexis Grewal, who brought the United States its first win in cycling in 1984, is of Indian descent.

There are many, many other Indians who have reached the top in their professions and have positions of respect and responsibility. India is proud of the achievements of its people in America. Prime Minister Indira Gandhi calls them "India's permanent ambassadors to the rest of the world."

Because they are educated and speak English well, Indian immigrants adjust easily to life in America. But because America is so big and busy, so different from India, newcomers often feel a little lost and lonely in the beginning. They are often torn between the two countries. Some Indian immigrants plan for years to return to India. Some do. Others try, but find they can no longer adjust to life in India and come back to America.

Over the years, Indian immigrants come to love America, with its well-ordered life and plenty of every-

Zubin Mehta, the musical director of the New York Philharmonic, is proud of his Indian roots and is still an Indian citizen.

thing. They appreciate the good things America offers them—free schools, free libraries, beautiful parks for their children to play in. Most of all, they are grateful because America has given them the chance to prove their worth and has rewarded their hard work. Before long, they learn American ways and make friends with the open and outgoing American people.

But Indians also enjoy being with other Indians, especially those who speak the same Indian language. Indians speaking the same language have formed many organizations all over the United States. These organizations hold weekend meetings, sponsor plays and talent shows in the regional language, and celebrate important festivals. Every year hundreds of Bengalis drive long distances to New York for Durga Puja. Those who love Hindi literature attend the meetings and poetry readings held by the International Hindi Association.

Associations based on religion have been formed, too. New York and other large cities have several Hindu temples. Yuba City, California has many gurudwaras for its large Sikh population. Jains, Parsees, and Muslims also have their associations and places of worship.

When famous Indian musicians like Ravi Shankar and Lata Mangeshkar perform in the United States, Bengalis, Punjabis, Hindus, and Muslims alike flock to hear them. Centers that work to make Indian music and culture more well known are being set up in American cities.

Sometimes groups of parents get together and hire dance and music teachers for their children, or take turns in teaching the language. Indian parents want their children to keep in touch with Indian culture. They want them to know about Asoka and Akbar, Rama and Krishna, Diwali and Pongal. They are afraid that children brought up in America will forget Indian values like obedience to parents and respect for elders. They worry about losing their Indian-ness.

But children born and raised in America want to be like the children they go to school with. Some feel that by keeping Indian traditions they become less American. And that is what they want more than anything else—to be American.

However, it is possible to be both Indian and American. Indians have had long experience in living side by side with people of different races and religions. In a sense, they have come from one melting pot to another. In India, Bengalis, Punjabis, Hindus, and Muslims are beginning to see themselves as just another type of Indian. In America, Indians are learning to think of themselves as yet another kind of American.

Children are taught the languages and culture of India in such places as the India School in Maryland.

Because they have arrived so recently, immigrants from India are learning what every American immigrant has had to learn: how to become American without losing themselves. How to keep one's traditions without clinging to them. How to face the future without forgetting the past.

But people cannot change overnight. It takes time for some to realize that they can celebrate Thanksgiving *and* Diwali, wear saris *and* skirts, enjoy curries *and* cook-outs. Some families continue to wear only Indian clothes and eat Indian food, while others become quite Americanized. Every family has its own way of adapting to American life, but Indian-American families also have many things in common.

Like these Indian children, American children of Indian descent often study the classical instruments and dances of India.

Indian-Americans like to live in large homes and own all the latest gadgets such as microwave ovens, computers, and video recorders. They love to have parties, and as often as possible, children are included in their parties. Indian-Americans remain people with close family ties. They seldom travel anywhere without their children. Together they often go to other cities to visit other Indian families. When Indian families get together, they discuss the latest news from India, eat Indian food, and watch Indian movies on videocassettes which they rent from the local Indian store.

Large American cities have several Indian grocery stores where one can buy spices, dals, frozen rotis, and sherbets. They carry Indian movie cassettes, Indian records, rakhis, incense, and pictures of Rama and Saraswati. Some stores specialize in saris made of American or Japanese fabric. Others carry popular gift items, like 220-volt appliances which can be used in India.

Indian restaurants have sprung up in several large cities. Some serve vegetarian foods. Others specialize in tandoori chicken, meat curries, and other north Indian favorites. Just as Americans have learned to love Italian pizza and Chinese chow mein, they are learning to enjoy Indian curries.

Indians have introduced many other things to America besides their food. In the summertime American stores are full of cotton clothes made in India. Yoga and meditation have helped many Americans lead calmer, healthier lives. Some Americans, looking for a different way of life, have turned to Indian thought and religion. The *Bhagavad Gita* greatly influenced American thinkers like Ralph Waldo Emerson and Henry Thoreau.

Americans learn Indian music at Berkeley University in California. Sitarist Ravi Shankar taught American audiences to love Indian music. Maestro Zubin Mehta took the Los Angeles Philharmonic to play for audiences in India. Recently, Ravi Shankar and Zubin Mehta worked together to produce *Rag*

Mala, a composition for sitar and orchestra that is a mixture of Eastern and Western musical ideas.

Before airplanes and television, ideas and people could travel only slowly from one country to another. Because travel was so dangerous and expensive, early American immigrants had to cut their ties with their homeland. But today, jet travel and telecommunications have made it possible for Indian immigrants to keep in touch with India.

Anita was three years old when she first visited India. She had never met her grandparents or her uncles or aunts before that. A crowd of relatives gathered to greet her when she arrived at New Delhi airport. Anita was handed from person to person and hugged, kissed, and cried over. At first it was a bit confusing for the tired little traveler from the other side of the world. She soon realized that she was a very important person.

She went everywhere with her parents. People were delighted by her American accent and foreign ways. They fussed over her and listened to every word she said, and gave her many gifts. And Anita brought many gifts from America—saris, lipsticks, perfumes, electrical appliances, and chewing gum.

Anita has gone back to visit India many times. Because she sees that nation from afar, she notices the changes that have taken place in India. The roads seem wider, the buildings bigger. The poor seem less poor than before. Even Grandma's cook likes to wear American jeans and an imported wristwatch. And because she lives among family and relatives, she sees the Indian people up close.

To see a nation from near and also from far is an experience most adults do not get. It gives you a chance to see that from far, cultures seem different, but up close, people are the same wherever they live.

Children like Anita are very special. They are part of a new generation, the jet generation. They travel across the ocean as infants and toddlers. They see the world from the sky. They will grow up knowing two different worlds, two different ways of life.

Like Ravi Shankar and Zubin Mehta, who also went abroad as youngsters, these children will help blend the two worlds together, the old and the new, the East and the West. They are like little ambassadors flying back and forth across the seas. In their suitcases, they bring a little bit of America to share with cousins in India. And when they return, they bring in their hearts and in their thoughts a little bit of India. When they grow up they will be a combination of the two ways of life—the Indian and American.

Already, as you can see, the other side of the world is not that different or that far away after all.

Appendix A
Indian Embassies and Consulates in the United States and Canada

The Indian embassies and consulates in the United States and Canada want to help Americans and Canadians understand Indian ways. For more information and resource materials about India, contact the embassy or consulate nearest you.

U. S. Consulates and Embassies

Chicago, Illinois
　Consulate General of India
　230 North Michigan Avenue
　Chicago, Illinois 60601
　Phone (312) 726-0659

Cleveland, Ohio
　Consulate of India
　1144 Union Commerce Building
　Cleveland, Ohio 44115
　Phone (216) 696-1144

Honolulu, Hawaii
　Consulate of India
　2051 Young Street
　P.O. Box 15638
　Honolulu, Hawaii 96815
　Phone (808) 947-2618

Houston, Texas
　Consulate of India
　P.O. Box 19756
　Houston, Texas 77024
　Phone (713) 747-6753

New Orleans, Louisiana
　Consulate General of India
　225 Baronnet
　New Orleans, Louisiana 70112
　Phone (504) 581-6641

New York, New York
　Consulate General of India
　3 East 64th Street
　New York, New York 10021
　Phone (212) 879-7800

　Permanent Mission of India
　　to the United Nations
　750 3rd Avenue, 21st Floor
　New York, New York 10017
　Phone (212) 661-8020

San Francisco, California
　Consulate General of India
　540 Arguello Boulevard
　San Francisco, California 94118
　Phone (415) 668-0662

Seattle, Washington
    Consulate of India
    Clinton, Fleck, Glein & Brown
    2112 3rd Avenue, Suite 500
    Seattle, Washington 98121
    Phone (206) 624-6831

Washington, D.C.
    Embassy of India
    2107 Massachusetts Avenue, N.W.
    Washington, D.C. 20008
    Phone (202) 939-7000

Canadian Consulates

Ottawa, Ontario
    High Commission of India
    10 Springfield Road
    Ottawa, Ontario K1M1C9
    Phone (613) 744-3751

Toronto, Ontario
    Suite 2920, Hudson Bay Center
    2 Bloor Street East
    Toronto, Ontario M4W1AS
    Phone (416) 960-0751

Vancouver, British Columbia
    Consulate General of India
    325 Howe Street
    Vancouver, B.C. Canada V6C1Z7
    Phone (604) 681-0644

Appendix B
The Languages of India

Though the people of India speak many tongues, most Indian languages can be divided into two groups. The north-Indian languages are called Indo-Aryan or Indo-European. The languages of southern India belong to the Dravidian group of languages.

Of the fifteen major languages recognized by the Indian constitution, Hindi is the single most popular one; it is spoken by about one-third of the population. This is why Hindi was selected to be the national language of India. It comes from Sanskrit, an ancient language used mainly by priests and scholars, because the holy books of the Hindus are written in Sanskrit.

Hindi has a well-developed grammar and vocabulary. Words are pronounced exactly as they are written. This is because the Hindi alphabet has thirteen vowels and thirty-six consonants. Hindi and Sanskrit are written in the same script, but there are many different scripts in use in India today. In fact, Urdu, which sounds very much like Hindi, has more Persian words and is written in Persian script. Together, Hindi and Urdu are the third most widely spoken languages in the world, after Chinese and English.

The languages of the world can be grouped into about eleven language families. Of these, the Indo-European and the Sino-Tibetan are the most important. Although most Asians speak the Sino-Tibetan languages, two out of three Indians speak Indo-Aryan languages, which are a branch of the Indo-European family. Dravidian languages like Tamil, Telegu, Kannada, and Malyalam are spoken by one-fourth of all Indians.

A Note About the Aryan Languages

When people hear the word Aryan, they think immediately of the Nazi dictator, Hitler, who used the term to describe a superior race. Actually, the term *Aryan* describes a group of languages rather than a race of people.

For many years European scholars studied the relationships between languages like Sanskrit, Latin, German, Greek, and English. Some thought that all European languages originated in Sanskrit. Later, research showed that all these languages had a common source—a prehistoric language they called Proto-Indo-European. This language was spoken around 5,000 B.C. It later gave rise to several different language groups, including Italic (Italian, Spanish, French, Latin, etc.), Hellenic (Greek), and Indo-Iranian groups. Those who spoke the Indo-Iranian or Indo-Aryan group of languages came to be called the Aryans.

Thousands of modern English words can be shown to come from some fifteen hundred Indo-European root words. Although English and Hindi sound completely different from each other, here are some words that show the similarity between the languages.

English	Proto-Indo-European	Sanskrit	Hindi
Mother	Mater	Mata	Mata
Father	Pater	Pita	Pita
Brother	Bhrater	Bhrata	Bhai
man	manu	manu	manav
mind	men		mun
wed	wadh (pledge)		wadha (promise)
nose	nas		nak
lip	leb		lubh
cow	gwou	go	gow
door	dhwer		dwar

Glossary

Note: the listed words are either Hindi or Sanskrit words unless another language is indicated.

ahimsa—nonviolence
Ahura Mazda—(Avestan) "Wise Spirit"; Zoroastrian name for God
Allah—(Arabic) Muslim name for God
Aryan—a group of languages that came from the prehistoric Proto-Indo-European language; also, the people who spoke those languages
avatar—birth of a god in human form
baraat—procession of a bridegroom's relatives as they follow him to his wedding
barfi—square candy made from milk
bazaar—(Persian) a busy marketplace
Bhagavad Gita—a holy book of the Hindus
bindi—a dot of makeup powder worn in the center of the forehead by girls and women
Brahma—the creator; one of the three main Hindu gods

Brahmin—member of the highest Hindu caste; usually a priest or scholar

Buddha/Buddhism—Buddha founded the religion Buddhism around 500 B.C.; Buddhism says that, to become wise, people must give up worldly desires and lead humble, thoughtful, patient lives

caste—(Portuguese) a social class or grouping of people based on occupation; Hindu society has four main castes with many smaller groups within each caste

charpie—a cot that has a wooden frame and a woven-rope "mattress"

chulha—stove

curry—(Tamil) a dish made with a sauce and seasoned with a blend of spices, often hot

dal—lentil soup; main source of protein for many Indians

Devi—the mother goddess; wife of Shiva

dhobi—washerman; *dho* means "wash"

dhoti—Indian men's clothing made by wrapping fabric around the waist and between the legs

Dravidian—a group of languages spoken in southern India

Gandhi, Mrs. Indira (1917-   )—a prime minister of India; daughter of Nehru

Gandhi, Mohandas (1869-1948)—leader of the Indian freedom movement in the 1900s; also called

Mahatma, "great soul"
Ganesh—elephant-headed god of wisdom and success
guru—teacher; *guru-bhakti* is devotion to a teacher
gurudwara—a Sikh temple
Guru Granth Sahib—holy book of the Sikhs
halwa—sweet pudding usually made from cereal
Harijan—"People of God;" the official name for untouchables, Hindus with no caste
Hindi—(from Persian) the national language of India
Hindu/Hinduism—a Hindu practices the religion Hinduism; in general, Hindus believe in laws and customs *(dharma)*, in reincarnation or rebirth, and in honoring their many gods by prayer and pilgrimages
Hindustan—(Persian) "Land of the Hindus;" old name for India
Islam—a religion begun by Muhammed; Islam teaches that there is one God; Muslims (followers of Islam) pray five times every day, travel to Mecca, their holy city, at least once in their lives, and view death as the start of eternal life in heaven
Jain/Jainism—a Jain practices Jainism, a religion begun by Mahavira; Jains believe each living thing contains a soul; therefore they eat no meat and try not to kill any living thing; they worship many gods but do not believe in a supreme god
Janam Patri—birth chart or horoscope

jizya—(Arabic) a tax collected by Muslim rulers from their non-Muslim subjects

Kabbaddi—an Indian team sport somewhat like our game of tag

kameez—long knee-length shirt

karma—action or deed; what you do in your present life determines your birth in your next life

kismet—(Turkish) fate or destiny

Koran—(Arabic) holy book of Islam

Krishna—the eighth avatar of Vishnu; a great warrior and hero worshipped by Hindus

Kshatriya—member of the second highest Hindu caste; they were typically soldiers and rulers; *ksatra* means "rule" in Sanskrit

laddoo—golden yellow, sweet balls of candy

Lakshmi—goddess of wealth; wife of Vishnu

Mahabharata—the longest poem in the world; it describes a war fought between 1000 and 700 B.C. and contains the *Bhagavad Gita*, a holy Hindu book

Mahavira—Founder of Jainism

maidan—field or playground

Mama—mother's brother; uncle

Manipuri—a dance from Manipur; of Manipur in northeastern India

mata—mother

mela—fair or carnival

mosque—(French, from Arabic root) place of worship for Muslims

Muhammed (570?-632 A.D.)—founder of Islam

Muslim—(Arabic) follower of Islam; also called a Mohammedan

Nanak, Guru (1469-1539)—founder of Sikhism

Namaste—Sanskrit for "I bow my head to you;" used both as greeting and farewell

Nehru, Jawahar Lal (1889-1964)—first prime minister of India

panchamrit—(Marathi) a food offering to the gods

Panchatantra—collection of Indian fables

panchayat—group of village leaders who make decisions and settle quarrels

panir—cheese made from curdled milk

paranthas—fried roti

Parsees—(Persian) people who came to India from Pars, Persia; Zoroastrians

Persia—an ancient empire that included what is now Iran and Afghanistan

pongal—(Tamil) a harvest festival in Tamil Nadu; pongal means "overflow"

pradesh—state or province

puja—prayer or worship

purdah—curtain or screen; also, a custom in which women keep their faces covered in front of men

Raavan—the ten-headed king of Lanka, a character

in the *Ramayana*

raita—yoghurt dish containing shredded vegetables

raja—king

Rajputs—warrior kings who once ruled parts of northern India, especially Rajasthan

Rama—seventh avatar of Vishnu, the hero of the *Ramayana*

Ramayana—Sanskrit epic that tells the story of Rama

roti—a pancake-like, flat bread

sambhar—spicy lentil soup containing vegetables

Sanskrit—an ancient language of India from which most modern Indian languages come

Saraswati—goddess of learning; wife of Brahma

sari—Indian women's garment made by wrapping fabric around the body

Shiva—the god of destruction; one of the three main Hindu gods

Shudra—a member of the fourth or lowest Hindu caste; mostly laborers

Sikh/Sikhism—a Sikh believes in Sikhism, a religion begun by Guru Nanak in the 1500s; Sikhism combines some Muslim beliefs with Hindu beliefs

sitar—a tall, long-stringed musical instrument somewhat like a lute

Skanda—six-headed Hindu god

tablas—a pair of bongo-like drums

tandoor—a clay oven

thali—a large, rimmed metal plate

Vaishya—a member of the third highest Hindu caste; typically traders and merchants

Vedas—four ancient sacred Hindu books

Vishnu—the preserver; one of the three main Hindu gods; see Krishna and Rama

yoga—ancient system of exercise meant to unite the body and the mind; *yog* is "yoking" or "union" in Sanskrit

Zend Avesta—sacred book of the Zoroastrian religion

Zoroastrian/Zoroastrianism—Zoroastrians practice Zoroastrianism, a religion begun in Persia by Zoroaster (Zarathustra); Zoroastrians believe that life represents a battle between good (the Supreme Being) and evil (His enemy)

Selected Bibliography

Beach, Milo Cleveland. *The Adventures of Rama,* with illustrations from a sixteenth-century Mughal manuscript. Freer Gallery of Art, Smithsonian Institution, 1983.

Davar, Ashok. *The Wheel of King Asoka.* Follett, 1977.

Gaer, Joseph. *The Adventures of Rama.* Boston: Little, Brown & Co., 1954

———*The Fables of India.* Boston: Little, Brown & Co., 1955.

Galbraith, Catherine and Rama Metha. *India Now and Through Time.* Dodd, 1971

Grant, Eva. *A Cow for Java.* New York: Coward, McCann & Geoghegan, 1973.

Haviland, Virginia. *Told in India: Favorite Fairy Tales.* Boston: Little, Brown & Co., 1973

Hewes, Agnes D. *Spice Ho!* New York: Knopf, 1941.

Masani, Shakuntala. *Gandhi's Story.* Walck, 1950.

Ryder, Arthur W. (translator). *The Panchatantra.* Chicago: University of Chicago Press, 1925.

Sommerfelt, Aimee. *The Road to Agra.* Criterion, 1961.

Spencer, Cornelia. *Made in India: The Story of India's People and of their Gifts to the World.* Knopf, 1953.

Many children's books about India have been published in India. The two books listed below are the best known.

Dhar, Shiela. *This India.* International Publications Service, 1974.
    _____*Children's History of India.* Seventh edition. Ind-US Inc.

For further information about these and other children's books about India you can write to:
  India School
  5502 Durbin Road
  Bethesda, MD 20814

Index

Agra, 22, 37
ahmisa, 28, 68
Ahura Mazda, 68
Akbar, 37
Alexander (the Great), 29
Allah, 67
Amritsar, 41, 50, 68
Andhra Pradesh, 9, 69, 93
Arjuna, 82, 123
army, Indian, 50, 68
Aryans, 26, 72
Asian Games, 134
Asoka, 30
Assam, 9, 13, 50, 51
Aurangzeb, 38
Babur, 36-37
badminton, 137
Bains, Didar Singh, 149
Bangalore, 24
Bangla Desh, 44, 50
baraat, 102
bazaar, 20
Bengal, 54, 97, 150
Bhagavad Gita, 156
Bharat, 76-77
Bharat Natyam, 55, 57
bindi, 59
Bombay, 22, 36, 40
books, 120-121
Bourlag, Norman, 18
Brahma, 72, 74
Brahman, 71
Brahmins (caste), 16, 26, 116
British Empire: India as part of, 40; India gains independence from, 43
Buddha, 27, 30, 68, 87-88

Buddhism, 28, 30, 68
Calcutta, 22, 40
calendar, lunar, 87-88
castes, 16-17, 26-27, 67, 144
ceremonies: *Amrit Chakana*, 101; *Bismillah*, 101; *Dastar Bandi*, 101; *Mundan*, 101; *Naamkaran*, 101; *Navjot*, 101; *Raksha Bandan*, 99; *Roza Rakha*, 101; weddings, 101-102
Ceylon (Sri Lanka), 30, 78
Chandragupta (Maurya), 29-30
Chandrasekhar, Dr. Subrahmanyan, 150
chappattis, 109; recipe for, 113-114
charpie, 106
Cherrapunji, 13
chess, 138
churidar pajamas, 58
clothing, 42, 57-59, 124
Columbus, Christopher, 148
curry, 108
daGama, Vasco, 36
dal, 109
dances, 55, 57
Dasrath, 76-77
Deccan plateau, 13
Delhi, 22, 86, 96, 98, 134, 157
democracy, 46-48
Desai, Morarji, 48
dhobis, 107
dhoti, 58
Dhritarashtra, 82
Diwali, 86, 153-154
Dravidians, 26
Dronacharya, 82, 123
East India Company, 40
education, non-traditional, 118. *See also* schools

Eklavya, 123
Emerson, Ralph Waldo, 156
fables, 71-84
farming, 13, 14, 15, 18, 26, 45, 54
family, 59-61, 99-100, 103, 157
festivals: *Baisakhi*, 92; *Basant*, 90; *Dassera*, 97; *Durga Puja*, 97, 152; *Ganesh Chaturthi*, 95; *Holi*, 90; *Janam Ashtami*, 93-95; Karnataka's doll, 97-98; *Lohri*, 90; *Navroze*, 92; *Onam*, 95; *Pongal*, 89; *Raksha Bandhan*, 99
foods, 109
games, 135-138, 141
Gandhi, Indira, 12, 46-48, 50, 151
Gandhi, Mohandas (Mahatma), 17, 42, 46, 55, 69
Ganesh, 73-74
Ganges River, 12-13, 92-93
Ghadar, 146
gitta, 141
gods, 26, 71-76
gopis, 81
government, 11-12
"Green Revolution," 45, 49
greetings, Indian, 60-61
Grewal, Alexis, 150
Gujarat, 9
gulli-danda, 141
Gupta kings, 31-32
guru, 36, 67, 116, 123
gurudwaras, 68, 88, 152
Guru Granth Sahib, 68
hairstyles, 58
halwa, 95, 109
Hanuman, 78
Harijans, 17
Harsha, 32
Harappa, 25
Himalayan Mountains, 12

Hindi, 10, 127, 152
Hindu, 10, 20, 24, 26, 33, 35-38, 40, 42, 44, 50, 62, 65, 67, 69-70, 72-75, 86, 92, 101, 109, 111, 144, 152-153
Hinduism, 10, 26-27, 35
holidays: birthday of India (Independence Day), 96-97; birthday of Guru Nanak, 88; *Buddha Purnima*, 87-88; Christmas, 87; *Diwali*, 86; *Id-ul-Fitr*, 88; *Mahavir Jayanti*, 88; Republic Day, 96
homemaking, 106-108; 111-113
horse sacrifice, 31
housing, 104-106
Huns, 32-33
immigration, Indian: adjustment after, 151-152, 154-155; early difficulties in, 145-147; reasons for, 149; settlements after, 149
Indian, confusion over term, 148
Indo-Gangetic plain, 13, 26
industry, 14, 24
International Hindi Association, 152
Islam, 32-33, 35, 67. *See also* Muslims
jackal, blue (fable), 84
Jains, 28, 68-69, 148, 152
Janam Patri, 62
Jews, 30-31, 67
ji, 61, 123
jizya, 37, 38
Kabbaddi, 135
Kabir, 35-36
kameez, 58
karma, 65, 67
Karnataka, 55, 97-98
Kashmir, 12, 44, 51
Kaurava, 82
Kerala, 14, 30, 55, 95-96, 148
Khan, Ustad Allauddin, 123
kho, 135
Khorana, Dr. Har Gobind, 127, 150

kismet, 62
Kohinoor, 38
Koran, 67, 101
Krishna, 80-83, 90, 93-95, 153
Kshatriyas, 16, 116
Kumbh Mela, 92-93
laddoos, 62, 85
Lakshadweep Islands, 7
Lakshman, 76-80
Lakshmi, 74
Lal, Gobind Behari, 150
languages, 10, 127
Lok Sabha (House of the People), 11
lungis, 58
Madras, 22, 40
Mahabali, 95
Mahabharata, 81, 122
mahals, 22
Maharashtra, 14, 55, 95
Mahavira, 28-29, 68
Mahmud, 33
maidan, 130
Mangeshkar, Lata, 9, 54, 152
Manipuri, 55
Marathas, 38
mathematics, origin of, 31
Mauryan kings, 29-30
Mehta, Ved, 150
Mehta, Zubin, 150, 156, 158
melas, 92, 93
Mohenjo Daro, 25
monsoons, 15
mosques, 65
movies, Indian, 21, 156
Mughal rulers, 37-38
Muhammed (prophet), 32
Muhammed of Ghori, 34
Muslims, 10, 32-37, 40, 42, 44, 50, 54, 65, 67, 69-70, 88, 101, 109, 111, 148, 152-153

myths, 72
names, Indian, 54
Nanak, Guru, 36, 67, 88
Nanda Devi, 12
Nehru, Jawahar Lal, 42, 45-47, 127, 133
Nicobar Islands, 7
non-alignment movement, 45
non-cooperation, 42
Pakistan, 10, 33, 42, 44, 47
Panchatantra, 84
panchayat, 46
Pandava, 82, 123
panir, 110
paranthas, 109
Parcheesi, 138
Parsees, 92, 150, 152
Patel, Sardar, 44
pilgrimages, 93
polo, 137
poona, 137
population, 7, 43
puggree, 101
puja, 67, 86, 97, 152
pulu, 137
Punjab, 18, 36, 50-51, 54, 89
purdah, 59
Qutab Minar, 34
Raavan, 78
Rag Mala, 156-157
raita, 111; recipe for, 115
rajas, 22
Rajasthan, 13, 22
Rajputs, 33-34, 37
Rajya Sabha (Council of States), 11
rakhi, 99
Rama, 76-80, 153
Ramadan, 88
Raman, C.V., 55
Ramayana, 76, 79

Ramleela, 98
religions, 10, 65-69
rickshaw, 20
roti, 109
sambhar, 109
Samadragupta, 31
Sanskrit, 26, 31-32, 35, 60, 74, 127
sari, 58, 154
Saund, Dalip Singh, 146
schools: ancient, 116; colleges, 128; city, 120, 124-124; convent, 124; government programs for, 118; rules in, 124-125; secondary, 128; sport in, 125, 134; supplies, 121; teachers, 122; tests in, 129; village, 120, 127
seasons, 15
Shah Jahan, 38
Shankar, Ravi, 54, 123, 152, 156, 158
Shastri, Lal Bahadur, 47
Shiva, 72-74
Shiva ji, 38
Shudras, 16
Sikhs, 10, 36, 38, 40, 50, 65, 67-69, 101, 145, 148, 152
silk, 14, 36
Sita, 77-80
sitar, 57, 123, 157

Sri Lanka (Ceylon), 7, 30, 144
spices, 14, 36, 108-109
sports: cricket, 130-133; field hockey, 133; school teams, 134; soccer, 133
Srinagar, 23
Tagore, Rabindranath, 54
Taj Mahal, 22, 38
Tamil Nadu, 9, 55, 69, 89, 150
Tandon, S. L., 150
tandoor, 109
Telegu, 35
textiles, 14
thalis, 111
Thoreau, Henry, 156
tonga, 20
Uttar Pradesh, 9, 54, 56, 69
Vaishyas, 16
Vedas, 26
veena, 74
Vijaynagar, 34
Vikramaditya, 31-32
Vishnu, 72, 74-75, 80, 95
wars: with China, 44; with Pakistan, 44, 47; revolution of 1857, 40
yoga, 138
Zend Avesta, 68
Zoroastrians, 10, 68, 92, 101

About the Author

Amita Vohra Sarin is a person of two worlds—the India in which she grew up and the United States to which she immigrated. In this book, her first for children, she wanted to show the India that shaped Indian immigrants and that still lives in their hearts.

Mrs. Sarin grew up and went to school in New Delhi, and received a master's degree in child development from Delhi University. She, her husband, and their children live in the Washington, D.C. area. Her brother and sisters have also settled in Washington, but the whole family travels frequently to India to see parents and other relatives.

By writing this book Amita Sarin wished to introduce American children to the richness of India's culture and history, and hopes that the children will wish to find out more about this fascinating country.

Photographer Stella Snead, who contributed many of the photos used in this book, began her career in photography in 1956 after some years as a painter. She lived in India for eleven years, photographing the people and art of the country. Her work has been shown in exhibits in India, Great Britain, and the United States. Ms. Snead's home is now in New York City.